SEASON OF THE WARRIOR

A POETIC TRIBUTE TO WARRIORS

BY

Joseph J. Truncale

ISBN: 1-4140-2509-2 (e-book)
ISBN: 1-4140-2508-4 (Paperback)
ISBN: 1-4140-2764-8 (Dust Jacket)

This book is printed on acid free paper.

Note: Some of the material in this poem collection has been privately published in the past in April of 1996 in Mr. Joseph J. Truncale's A Poetic Tribute To Warriors Collection and in A Tribute to Warriors: A Haiku Collection.

1stBooks - rev. 11/24/03

DEDICATION

This book is dedicated to my wife Carol, whose love, support, loyalty and understanding of my warrior life style, has given me great happiness and inner peace.

To my son Brian and Daughter Michelle, who have given us much love and joy.

Finally, this book was written to honor all those who live the way of the warrior and follow the code of Bushido, past, present and future. To those who follow this most difficult path, push on my friends, for your cause is just and honorable.

TABLE OF CONTENTS

INTRODUCTION

****

Foster and polish
The warrior spirit
While serving the world;
Illuminate the Path
According to your inner light.

Morihei Ueshiba

****

INTRODUCTION

Our fasination with warrior ways is universal in scope and spans all cultures, races and historic times. Every country has had its warrior heroes, and it has been said that warriors are the embodiment of life itself. This poetic tribute attempts to reach into the very heart and soul of the warrior, which is more rich and deep than most people can imagine. The warrior way is the most difficult of paths to follow. The challenges and obstacles are more than the average individual can comprehend. The warrior thinks differently than the average person about gaining and achieving values. They follow codes and philosophies that guide their conduct and actions. Their weapons and tactics can change with history, but their heart and soul remains true to their code.

What most people think of, when they hear the term warrior, often comes from the simplistic definitions found in most common dictionaries. For example, the Oxford American Dictionary comes up with this definition. "A person who fights in battle, a member of the armed services." Webster's Dictionary says a warrior is;"One who fights in a war or battle." The Random House American College Dictionary also does little to enlighten us on what exactly is a warrior? "A man engaged or experienced in warfare; soldier." The truth is, in our modern society, these definitions are at best, incomplete.

To obtain a true picture of the warrior we must look to other more accurate and complete interpretations. For example, when investigating the Japanese Samurai, the term Bushi is used. The break down of that term is as follows: "Bu consists of bun: This refers to "literature or letters, and generally arts of peace) stopping the spear. Bu also prohibits violence and subdues weapons...it puts people at peace, and harmonizes the masses."(From Ideals of the Samurai). Shi refers to someone who obtained their rank through a process of learning. In early Japan this included the professions of farmers, craftsmen and tradesmen.

The term Bushi in ancient Japan was reserved for those men and women warriors of nobility. They were educated in the literary arts, as well as the fighting systems. Their profession demanded both a disciplined mind and body. Many Bushi (warriors) were also poets, who often wrote down their thoughts before a battle, and after a battle, if they survived. They balanced literary skills with the warrior arts. They followed a code called Bushido, which means "The Way of the Warrior." The same nobility status was recognized in the European warrior class, when a brave soldier was awarded the rank of knight. Again, they also followed an unwritten code of conduct that marked them above the average person. The brave, courageous and courteous qualities of the European Knight followed the same path of honor as the

Japanese Bushi. The U.S. Armed Services use the term "Officer and a Gentleman" to emphasize the importance of honor. It is the same code of conduct philosophy that was followed by warrior leaders in the past.
As Schlegel stated in his Philosophy of History, "Chivalry is itself the poetry of life."

In this series of poems, essays, codes and commentary, you will discover the very heart and soul of the warrior and the philosophy that guides their way of life and death.

Joseph J. Truncale
July 15, 2003

QUALITIES AND TRAITS OF THE WARRIOR

There are standards of conduct every true warrior must adhere to in order to be accepted as belonging to that noble class of individuals. One must look beyond the simplistic definitions of rectitude, courage, honor, politeness, honesty and self control as it applies to the warrior.

RECTITUDE: (JUSTICE)

A warrior views this more than just rightness in conduct. For the Samurai it meant the "power of resolution." As one Bushi defines it: "Rectitude is the power of deciding upon a certain course of conduct in accordance with reason, without wavering;-to die when it is right, to strike when to strike is right." In essence, rectitude for the warrior is acting valiantly for THE RIGHT REASONS. We can point to modern day warriors and see rectitude in action. One example is our law enforcement officers. Who, but an insane person, rushes to screams of someone with a gun. Indeed, police officers demonstrate rectitude by their response to possible dangerous situations and incidents. They do it for THE RIGHT REASONS, to protect the citizens they serve.

COURAGE:

For the follower of the warrior code, courage without the "cause of righteousness" is not thought of as a virtue. Reckless conduct is often confused with true bravery and valor. The warrior must act courageously for reasons that are proper and right. The development of courage for the ancient warriors began at a young age, where parents would assign dangerous tasks for their children to perform. The Samurai's son were sometimes deprived of food, made to walk in bare feet to school. Sometimes they were awakened in the early morning hours to deliver messages, and once or twice a month made to stay up all night. These rights of passage may seem cruel in our modern age, but these tests developed strict self control, which hopefully, turned into the kind of courage required to be an adult warrior. To act in spite of the odds against you, to be calm in the face of danger, to live, or die, because it is the right thing to do, are all part of the warrior's search for true courage.

RESPECT AND POLITENESS:

The traditional martial art schools demonstrate these essential qualities. The true warrior is at all times courteous to both superiors and subordinates. It is a sign of inner strength and confidence when one is respectful, polite and courteous. If you desire to see these qualities in action, visit a traditional martial arts school. You will find the most polite and courteous members are those of higher rank.

SEASON OF THE WARRIOR
A POETIC TRIBUTE TO WARRIORS

HONOR:

The warrior, above all things, exhibits the quality of honor. Honor refers to doing the right thing as it relates to your obligations. This is the very essence of honor. A warrior knows the importance of taking the high moral ground. Though saving face is a facet of warriorship, by itself it is not honor. True honor means doing a thing because of a just obligation.

TRUTHFULNESS:

Truthfulness is part of being an honorable person. The samurai warriors knew that real honesty is courage in action. The quality of truthfulness is tied directly to honor. The warrior views lying as highly dishonorable and has contempt for those who are not truthful. Indeed, honor and doing the RIGHT THING seems rare today, especially in our blame someone else society, where personal responsibility is a lost quality. The reason a criminal can never become a true warrior is because they lack individual truthfulness and honor.

RESTRAINT:

In all cultures, and at all times, warriors are considered dangerous people because of their combat skills and courage. The warrior has forged his/her body and mind to endure pain and discomfort. Indeed, the warrior is trained in the combat arts and can cut down an enemy in less than a second; but yet, they will exhibit courtesy, respect and restraint when dealing with the public. They exist to protect society from criminals, enemies of the country and other predators. Where the average person might allow fear to rule them during a physical threat, warriors thrust themselves into the action, determined to destroy the enemy. As I have often said, "The meek are only allowed to exist in peace because there are warriors who are willing to fight to protect them. The meek would be either slaves or slaughtered if it were not for warriors willing to do the right thing."

LOYALTY:

Another important aspect of being a true warrior is the quality of LOYALTY. Individuals who lack this trait can never be trusted. Whether it is a relative or supposedly friend, never trust a person who does not have the trait of loyalty. Loyalty refers to being true to one's honorable principles and philosophy. It means showing respect for parents, superiors, subordinates, teachers, instructors and fellow students. We have all known certain people whose loyalty was based upon greed rather than honor. The recognition of those who have shared their knowledge with us in the past and helped shape the person we have become today is all part of loyalty.

IT IS TO THESE WARRIOR QUALITIES THIS BOOK IS DEDICATED.

ENJOY.

SEASON OF THE WARRIOR

Cherry blossoms beginning to bloom,
The Bushi enjoys this spring noon,
Light winds brush across his face,
A good season to love and taste.

The heat of summer is so intense,
The warrior stops by a fence to rest,
Placing his sword close to his side,
Always ready to battle, live or die.

Falling leaves of red and gold,
His favorite season to walk so bold,
He picks up his Jo made of wood,
Cool breeze on his face feels so good.

Winter wind with snow so deep,
The warrior walks promises to keep,
All seasons are the warrior's home,
All his battles must be fought alone.

JJT.

THE PARENT MARTIAL ART

Everything must have a beginning,
All knowledge gained from same source,
Judo was not created in a vacuum,
Aikido did not come from thin air.

Karate came from the same parents,
As did Kobudo and other combat arts,
Original source of these systems,
Few people remember the past.

Developed during feudal times,
Its purpose was made for war,
Combat efficiency was its goal,
The cost in life took its toll.

What is the combat art so few know?
Many ancient styles died with the times,
Now systems recognize they are a part,
Jujitsu, the name of this parent art.

JJT

DAITO RYU

Ancient history a Jujitsu Ryu,
Tribute to a master long over due,
He traveled often all over Japan,
A member of an honored clan.

Sokaku Takeda, a samurai soul,
A master whose story was not told,
Like cherry blossoms with morning due,
Ancient samurai art lives, Daito-Ryu,

A hard style with combat goals,
A warrior spirit pure as gold,
Modern Budo masters owe so much,
Aikijutsu they all have touched.

Daito Ryu, a ghost from the past,
Master Takeda's art, sure to last,
A true master this poem honors,
The link between old and modern.

JJT

Joseph J. Truncale

LONELY WARRIOR HEART

To seek and not find,
To search in hopeless dispair,

To learn more without knowing,
To explore and find not peace,

To trust and be deceived,
To climb a mountain so high,

To run the swifter race,
To fight and lose again,

To leap in danger's path,
To jump into harm's way,

To rush forward with will alone,
To train even when tired,

To be courageous when odds are many,
To feel fear and just ignore,

To be calm in face of danger,
To walk alone and be at peace,

To wield the sword of justice,
To love deeply and be loved,

SEASON OF THE WARRIOR
A POETIC TRIBUTE TO WARRIORS

To face death in the eye and smile,
To live and die, the warrior's heart.

JJT

Joseph J. Truncale

WARRIOR'S CODE

Perspiration on their brow,
Like tears from ancient gods,
A life of toil and pain,
A call to arms they hear,

Never give in to hopeless doubt,
To survive is what this is about,
The warrior knows he must fight,
Because his cause is just and right,

Training to win the battle,
This is the life he chooses to live,
It matters not the pain he feels,
The warrior will refuse to kneel,

Bruises and scars badges of courage,
Driving ever forward to his glory,
He will not forsake his noble quest,
His code of Bushido put to the test.

JJT

MASTER GICHIN FUNAKOSHI (1868-1957)

The next poem was written to honor Master Gichin Funakoshi, who is considered the "father" of modern karate. Though he was not the only karate master to bring this art to Japan from his home in Okinawa; however, he was the first one invited to Japan in May of 1922 to give a karate demonstration. Master Jigoro Kano, the father of Judo, was impressed with Funakoshi's karate demonstration and invited him to teach at the Kodokan. The result was that Shotokan karate became one of the most popular traditional karate styles practiced around the world.

Joseph J. Truncale

THE SAMURAI SPIRIT WITHIN

White uniform so clean and pure,
Yells so loud as punches fly,
Brow is soaked with effort great,
Goal to enter elightened state.

Years of work to learn this art,
To lose oneself in moving Zen,
Always checking balance, stance,
Body moving, kata combat dance.

Master Funakoshi looks down from above,
Happy his art is practiced with love,
tradition demands disciplined study,
Rewards are great for those who endure.

Lightening hands and feet are weapons,
To block and defend make up the lessons,
Learning to fight in hopes of peace,
Defending the weak from predatory beasts.

Sweat and blood flowing onto white Gi,
Hard practice is heard with loud KIAs,
Students moving across the floor,
Rights of passage to Samurai's door.

JJT

MORIHEI UESHIBA (1883-1969)

Before Ueshiba founded his art of aikido, he was a student of one of the most famous warriors of that time. His name was Sokaku Takeda (1860-1943), and his fighting art is called Daito Ryu Aikijutsu. I have also honored him in my poem, "Daito Ryu." Ueshiba studied many warrior arts, but for many years he trained and helped teach with Sokaku Takeda. From this Aikijutsu art, Ueshiba researched the development of what he called Ki, which is a form of inner power. He developed one of the most beautiful martial arts, Aikido. This martial art appeals to those seeking a more esoteric approach to martial art study. Ueshiba, is honored by his students who refer to him as "O' Sensei, which means great teacher. This poem honors him and his art.

O'SENSEI

Mystic movements flowing water,
Old master smiles, attacker's fly,
Spirit of one with the universe,
Zen is always, never dies.

Gift from heaven O'sensei claims,
The Aikido art is his way,
Gentle man with warrior's heart,
To share with all, not apart.

Energy flows like tide in seas,
As the mind of the master leads,
Enemy and defender move as one,
Laughing master bright as the sun.

His goal to bring humanity together,
Beauty in motion, soft as a feather,
Calm warrior's art put to the test,
O'sensei's gift humankind's best.

The master's death brings such sorrow,
His students will keep him immortal,
All kneel and bow to honor his glory,
O'sensei lives on, the Aikido story.

JJT

KASHIMA SHENDIN JINKINSHIN KAGE RYU

The sword has always been a symbol of the warrior in many cultures. One of the oldest kenjutsu (way of the sword) styles in Japan is Kashima Shendin Jinkinshin Kage Ryu. They use a special wooden sword in their practice, which is called a Bokuto. This sword is thicker and heavier than the usual Bokken (Japanese wood sword) used in other Japanese styles. Though the cutting practice is the same in most styles of kenjutsu, the unique thing about Kashima Shendin Jinkinshin Kage Ryu is their practice of a kata (formalized form) called The Hojo. This sword kata is done by two people, and there are a total of 8 sections, which are broken down into the following: Kage Side: Spring, Summer, Fall and Winter. Shin Side: Spring, Summer, Fall and Winter. In combination with learning the movements of this kata, a special way to breathe is also practiced called Hojo Breathing.

THIS POEM HOPES TO HONOR THIS GREAT JAPANESE SWORD ART.

KASHIMA SWORD ART

Kashima Shrine held high above,
Followers practice this art with love,
Bokuto in hands instructor leading,
Across the floor Hojo breathing.

Shadow kata is called moving Zen,
Body kept straight with no bend,
Ancient sword art for soul healing,
Cut through the center of your being.

Spring opens in beginning light,
Alert to the rising sun, so bright,
Spirit of spring felt so deep,
Sword cuts through, clash and meet.

Summer comes riding on blazing sun,
Bold cut to center, battle is won,
Shin and Kage, moving together,
Intense focus, nothing is better.

Autumn breeze with leaves turning,
Meet the force with fires burning,
Follow Shin with each every move,
Courageous cut, nothing to prove.

SEASON OF THE WARRIOR
A POETIC TRIBUTE TO WARRIORS

Winter wind with snow on your blade,
Fluid pattern, a sword cut is made,
Sword rises, but comes down gentle,
Cut through your own being essential.

JJT

JIGORO KANO (1860-1938)

Master Kano was an educated man, and could write in both Japanese and English. He studied numerous styles of jujitsu, but his three primary teachers were Masamoto Iso of the Tenshin shin 'Yo Ryu, Tsunetoshi Iikubo of the Kito Ryu and Hachinosuke Fukuda of the Tenshin Shin'Yo Ryu. Master Kano saw the decline of interest and popularity in the warrior arts in Japan. He felt it was important to preserve the historical Japanese heritage in these arts. In order for the old jujitsu arts to become popular Kano knew there must be a more modern approach so that all people could practice it. In February of 1882 he founded the Kodokan, (Institute for study of the way). To show how from small things great things can be accomplished, the first year he opened the Kodokan Master Kano, who was only 22 years of age at the time, had only nine students. Today Judo is recognized as an Olympic sport and is practiced by thousands of people world wide.

This poem honors Master Kano and his Judo.

THE GENTLE WAY

Professor Kano watching from above,
The art of Judo he surely loves,
Students gliding on matted floor,
Flying bodies, white Gis are worn.

An art that's called the gentle way,
Ukemi practice begins each class,
Students learning to throw and fall,
Inside the Judo training hall.

A sport for warriors that is true,
To unbalance partner is the clue,
Players in white thrown on the mat,
sliding feet moving like a cat.

Learning to throw a technical skill,
To succeed, you must have a strong will,
Throwing is not all in this art,
Grappling and choking also a part.

Honor the masters teaching this art,
For they do it with a loving heart,
The art of Judo practiced this day,
This is Master Kano's gentle way.

JJT

Joseph J. Truncale

THE BATTLE OF FALL

Leaves of red falling drops of blood,
Landing at the base of a tree in mud,
Sword in hand his eyes gazing out to sea,
winning this battle was not to be.

A warrior has fought his final battle,
Too weak to mount his golden saddle,
Sinking down to the wet leaves of red,
He lays down to rest his tired head.

Brave first knight of King Arthur lays,
Unafraid to face his death this day,
Undefeated whenever his duty called,
Never thought he'd be the one to fall.

One final time he attempts to stand,
Ignoring the blood on his hands,
He feels his life slipping away,
Enter warrior's heaven this fall day.

JJT

THE MODERN WARRIOR

Young and old, training for survival,
For this is their worthy goal.

True warriors need not pretend or bully,
Because their skills are developed fully.

Facing death with a calm peaceful mind,
The warrior's code is never denied.

A love of life, but prepared to die,
Fighting evil people who always lie.

Warriors stride with cat like steps,
They try their best when put to the test.

A hatred of war but willing to fight,
To defeat barbarians in their sight.

Warriors will battle day and night,
For their cause is just and right.

JJT

THE STREET WARRIORS

Kevlar worn like ancient shields,
The street is their battle field,
Knights in blue with badges shining,
Honor bound to do their duty.

Society's defenders with loaded guns,
A police officer's job is never done,
Criminal's rights are of most concern,
Victims ignored, lessons are learned.

Code of honor to protect and serve,
Blue warriors with courageous nerve,
Swords worn like ancient samurai,
Blue steel weapons at their sides.

Predatory animals roam the streets,
To rob and steal victims they meet,
Thin blue line is all that's left,
Right of passage put to the test.

Officers rushing to scene in haste,
Never knowing what danger they face,
To survive the street is the goal,
Heart of the warrior in their soul.

JJT

WARRIOR'S RITE OF PASSAGE

Red shirts worn like honor's blood this week,
They come together with promises to keep,
Bodies racked with the pains of battle,
Training to survive, batons clash and rattle.

"Never give up." The cry of these brave souls,
The street is watching, eyes mean and cold.
To win the battle must be our goal,
Society demands we serve and be bold.

Long hours spent honing warrior skills,
To battle predators who test our will,
The warrior's heart can't be denied,
Never forgetting those who have died,

Criminals say the warriors are dead,
Officers know they must use their head,
Warriors come to train and learn,
Souls of fire that brightly burn.

JJT

Joseph J. Truncale

THE ZEN WARRIOR

To live and die is the same,
To battle strong be cunning,
To wield your sword from high,
Zen warrior fears not to die.

Seated Zazen to become calm,
Near blue water by a pond,
He senses the enemy is near,
Zen warrior feels no fear.

Flashing blade in the moon light,
Shadows creeping hiding from sight,
Serenely aware a rustle of leaves,
Zen warrior, eyes closed, but he sees.

The assassin almost upon him,
He smiles and feels the wind,
The enemy drawing his sword,
Zen warrior becomes reborn.

Death is felt this fall night,
One will die in this sword fight,
Assassin with sword over his head,
Zen warrior is faster, enemy is dead.

JJT

SAMURAI'S ART

Flashing steel glowing in the sun,
Warriors clash the battle is won,
The soul of the Bushi in his hands,
Drops of blood soak into the sand.

Learning to win but prepared to die,
The samurai code is to never lie,
Soul of the warrior is his sword,
This is the way he serves his lord.

Cherry blossoms in sunlight pink,
The Samurai's eyes never blink,
Spirit filled with ancient honor,
As the battle grows ever nearer.

Swinging the Katana from high above,
A cut is made through hand and glove,
His spirit is great sword cut to win,
A fatal head blow, Samurai yells MEN.

JJT

Joseph J. Truncale

SOUL OF THE WARRIOR

Sunlight blinding flash on steel blade,
The Bushi slowly cleans the soul of,
His inner being.

Placing his sword inside the scabbard,
He sits in Zazen silent meditation,
The morning battle is near.

Calmness of mind to face the enemy,
Birds singing their morning song,
Life and death the same.

Obligation to duty and honor bound,
The Katana placed inside his Obi,
Ready to face himself.

Cherry blossoms fill the sky today,
The Samurai welcomes the sweet scent,
A good day to live and die.

JJT

THE ROAD ALONE

Lonely hours of sweat and blood,
This is the price to pay,
A warrior's quest,
A grueling path,
Of countless hours today.

For what you say, the fools cry out,
To defeat your enemy is true,
The Warrior's code is clear,
Always do the right thing,
And never play for fools.

The rocky road of grit and pain,
And no one can take your place,
Scars of battle on your face,
A warrior always walks alone,
To face his battles small and great.

JJT

THE ANCIENT WARRIOR

His tired body keeps moving this night,
Youthful years past, old age in sight,
Why does this man keep practicing,
Performing his kata, survival dancing.

Answer is not with his still strong body,
For he still hears the warrior song,
Scared and bruised from battles in past,
He keeps moving, but not as fast.

Tired eyes that have seen too much pain,
He still believes there is much to gain,
Sword in hand, moving Zen his guide,
He'll never give up and will change the tide.

Why does this ancient warrior keep on,
Some say all his battles have been won,
There is one left, facing death so bold,
Because he has the Samurai soul.

JJT

WARRIOR WITH VISIONS OF MOUNT FUJI

White flakes of beauty floating down,
Foot prints in the snow only sound,
Grim Reaper sings in the bitter wind,
Samurai keeps moving, for he must win.

To die in battle a warrior's honor,
Code of Bushido, something to ponder,
Beautiful snow cap mountain of dreams,
Quiet woods, one can see a moon beam.

Mount Fuji in sight like calm Zen,
A fire in a cave of warrior's den,
Ancestors looking down from above,
Proud heritage a Samurai's love.

Tired warrior lays down his head,
Dreaming of Cherry blossoms so red,
Cold wind blowing covered with snow,
Road of the warrior paved in gold.

JJT

THE 300 SPARTANS

From birth trained in warrior skills,
Strong bodies and mind they will build,
The spear, the bow, and sword they learn,
Standing in line waiting their turn.

The fight is near, for this they know,
Spartan warriors look down from the knoll,
Prepare for the battle is their war cry,
They will fight bravely, unafraid to die.

Overwhelming forces begin their attack,
Only 300 brave Spartans to beat them back,
To guard the pass from invaders their goal,
They fight fiercely and are brave and bold.

They will lose this noble fight today,
But win the battle at sea in the bay,
Greece will fight bravely and win,
Their culture lives on even today.

JJT

ODEN'S WARRIORS

If one chooses the warrior way,
You will learn to labor all day,
A way of life not for the meek,
A warrior must be strong, not weak

A calm mind like gentle rain,
A noble quest is something to gain,
Spirits of war Gods in their soul,
Oden awaits them pockets of gold.

The quest for glory to be achieved,
The warrior way is what they believe,
Oden looks down gives them his blessing,
Viking warrior blade ready for testing.

Flaming arrows fill the night sky,
Some will live and some will die,
Sword in hand as death draws near,
Oden waits above, nothing to fear.

JJT

Joseph J. Truncale

THE SWEET SCIENCE

Smell of sweat and pounding bags,
Punches thrown a jaw is tagged,
Eye of the tiger shows its face,
Bobbing and weaving quicken pace.

Move and jab, bob and weave,
When in the ring a boxer can't leave,
Take a punch, give a punch,
Gloves strike, feel the crunch.

Speedy hands quick as a fox,
Lots of heart needed to box,
Courage great to take the hits,
A boxer must also use his wits.

At home in the ring, battle begins,
A boxer's goal is always to win,
Train for months preparing to fight,
The champion crown is in his sight.

JJT

THE YOUNG MASTER'S DREAM

Punches faster than the eye can see,
Thrown by a young master-Bruce Lee,
Always training to be the best,
Freedom from the classical mess.

Not concerned with traditional ways,
Bruce's Jeet Kune Do lives on today,
Adjust to your opponent being taught,
Total fighting skills always sought.

Learning the way of no way is hard,
Driving through an opponent's guard,
Speed and timing must be mastered,
Learn to move ever faster.

Don't be hung up on just a name,
Learning to fight is not a game,
Jeet Kune Do is the name it's called,
But Bruce insisted there be no walls.

Sad that Bruce Lee died so young.
His star was bright as the sun,
This combat art is alive and well,
So much to learn, so much to tell.

JJT

WOODEN SWORD PRACTICE

Bokken in hand a thousand cuts,
Daily practice always a must,
Moving forward, side and back.
Kata performed, counter attack.

Warrior art of ancient times,
Trust in sword but use your mind,
Eyes focus on imaginary foes,
Moving forward a cut that flows.

Warrior calm, but ready to strike,
The bokken is swung with all his might,
Hours perfecting Samurai skills,
A warrior knows one cut can kill.

He knows no one carries a sword today,
His code Bushido, the Kenjutsu way,
Modern warrior does not serve a lord,
Nevertheless, he still swings his sword.

JJT

THE SPIRIT OF THE BRAVE

Tested for manhood by his tribe,
Rite of passage no brave can hide,
Harsh, but needed to walk among men,
His culture demands it, as in Zen.

Riding his horse up mountains so high,
Indian brave looks at death in the eye,
Little bear hears the cold wind blowing,
He feels cold, but keeps on going.

A vision quest from ancient past,
Relatives now gone, he is the last,
Breathing hard from his mountain climb,
The warrior knows he is pressed for time.

Reaching the top he sees his goal,
Grabbing the feather as if it were gold,
Last test completed to become a brave,
Little bear spends the night in a cave.

JJT

Joseph J. Truncale

SPECIAL FORCES

Guerrilla fighting their specialty,
Hiding in the bush enemy can't see,
A call to arms to save the day,
Army Green Beret so bold and brave.

Marines always ready, first to fight,
Fire in their souls burn so bright,
Though there numbers are very few,
There is nothing they cannot do.

Whether on land, air and mighty seas,
The powerful Navy SEALS are kept busy,
Proven their bravery in many a fight,
Frogmen in black attack in the night.

Brave special forces of every branch,
Danger abound, but they take a chance,
Their righteous cause is always just,
This poetic tribute to them is a must.

JJT

A PSALM FOR WARRIORS

Battle songs singing in his heart,
Some say that war is merely an art,
The glory of life is conflict to win,
To be without courage is the sin.

His soul a melodious sweet chord,
In his hand he holds a battle sword,
War winds blowing in his face,
Walking in harms way to meet his fate.

A heart that's true and never lies,
His destiny is clear, he knows why,
All ages and times, warriors to call,
Brave men and women always stand tall.

Honor at stake will make us fight,
Enemies are on the hill in plain sight,
Battle lines drawn, swords raised high,
A good day to live, a good day to die.

JJT

SEASON OF THE WARRIOR
A POETIC TRIBUTE TO WARRIORS

HAIKU

Haiku is a uniquely Japanese poetic form. The person credited with creating this form of poetry is Matsuo Basho (1644-1694). Many Samurai also wrote this type of poetry. Originally I had written a separate poem collection of Haiku (Tribute to Warriors: A Haiku Collection, 1992), but I decided to add this Haiku collection to make this poetry collection more complete and meaningful. One of my black belt students, Carl Anderson, who has studied Jujitsu, Karate and Kobudo with me asked if he could write a few Haiku for me. He wanted to express his love of the "way of the warrior" through Haiku. The following four Haiku are expressed beautifully by him.

Shihan-Tired Warrior
Bushido lost in modern times
Must press on

Humbleness Bushido code
Swallowing pride chokes me
Better person

Weary teacher
Sit down-admire
Sempai makes you proud

Bujutsu devine gift
My mind cannot rest
Is this my path?

Carl Anderson

WHAT HAIKU MEANS TO ME

Since the creation of the written word, writers and poets have searched for the best way to express a thought, an image an idea or an emotion in as few words as possible. As a writer who has many varied interests, one of them being the martial arts, my fasination with things from the far east has led me on a journey of amazing discoveries, not just in the martial arts, but in many intriguing areas. My study of haiku, through reading, tapes and writing, has helped me to better understand my complex feelings and experiences. Putting them in the haiku form has enabled me to share them with readers in a way that is both meaningful and relevant. I have attempted to combine the traditional Japanese haiku form, and relate it to modern experiences in creating this haiku collection. Only you, the reader, who enjoys and appreciates haiku, can determine whether or not I have succeeded.

I have attempted through the medium of poetry, in this case haiku, to give an insight into my world when I was a police officer. Some of these haiku may seem a little gruesome, but to really appreciate the honey of life, one must also be willing to taste the bitter lemon of life. It is the Yin and Yang of life that makes it interesting. I have also included the traditional Japanese nature subjects in this poem collection.

Joseph J. Truncale

For me, haiku is a form of poetry that has taught me how to express my wide range of emotions and experiences to form an image the reader can grasp, see and feel. In some ways, haiku has allowed me to understand clearer, what the philosophy of Zen attempts to express in its teachings. To explore your inner being through reflection is what haiku accomplishes, but only if your open up your heart and mind.

Joseph J. Truncale

A BRIEF HISTORY OF HAIKU

The development of haiku cannot be talked about without understanding that haiku originally came from the popular renga poem forms. Renga are linking poems, which in Japan around the thirteenth century, was a very popular poetic form. At that time three or more poets would get together and have renga parties. At these gatherings one poet would start a poem and the other poets would take turns adding to the creation until they were satisfied. This could take quite a long time because some renga were as long as one thousand stanza. As William J. Higginson mentions in his text, The Haiku Handbook, "A typical renga from the thirteenth through the sixteenth centuries is fifty or one hundred stanzas long.

"The man most noted for creating haiku is Matsuo Basho (1644-1694). Basho was a teacher and master of renga. He would travel around the country teaching his technique of linked poems. Basho's method of creating images in a short poem has become known today as haiku. It is important to note, that Basho was not known for haiku when he created the form, but was famous for a type of renga known as "Haikai-no-renga," which translates into "humorous linked poem." Basho's starting verse in a poem he called hokku, because it was originally the starting verse of a renga. Mr. Basho was a master of all types of haikai, and is recognized as the writer who perfected this form. His most famous poem is as follows.

Old pond
a frog leaps in
water's sound

The Zen like quality of Japanese literature can be felt in this Basho creation.

Clouds occasionally
make a fellow relax
moon-viewing

In Japan they speak of the four great haiku masters. The first was Basho. The second is Yosa Buson (1716-1784), who was an artist and a poet. What a great artistic combination. His specialty was haiku, and he was greatly influenced by Basho. Buson could see poetry in every day normal life. This poem by Buson reflects his unique perspective.

A thief
vanishes over the roof tops
night chill

Kobayashi Issa (1762-1826) is the third great master of haiku. Issa was raised in the country and is admired among the Japanese people for his realistic approach to haiku. Issa was a complex individual, and though he is thought of by some to be pessimistic, in this author's view, Issa was a man who related to the reality of the times. These two poems provide an example of his haiku style.

the woman
leads into the mist-
low tide beach

morning-dew
morning glories he sells
rough fellow

The last of the four great masters of haiku is Masaoka Shiki (1867-1902), who is known as the first poet to actually use the term haiku. Shiki was not only a master of haiku, but also of another type of traditional Japanese poem called a Tanka. Even though Shiki only lived until he was thirty five years old, he is famous for starting new schools of writing, in both haiku and tanka. The following are two examples of Shiki's haiku poems.

The first one written reflects the battle field of ancient Japan.

The second poem was written while he was a war correspondent in China.

summer grass
those mighty warriors
dream tracks

Joseph J. Truncale

the pear blossoming
after the battle this
ruined house

From these four great masters of haiku came many other followers of this wonderful poetic form. Today, millions of Japanese, as well as thousands of people around the world, love to read and write haiku poems.

HAIKU FORM WRITTEN IN ENGLISH

Early writers of haiku in the west did not completely understand the Japanese language and began writing haiku using the seventeen syllable form, with lines of five-seven-five, to create a haiku form. However, the Japanese do not count syllables, but employ sound symbols called "onji." An onji is a short sound, which in the Japanese language is not the same thing as an English syllable. It was mistakenly believed by many western poets, that because the Japanese haiku is made up of seventeen onji, this would be the same thing as western syllables. It should be noted, however, that many excellent western poets created very good haiku using the seventeen syllable form. Nevertheless, to actually create a haiku form that equals the Japanese onji, a ten, twelve, of fifteen syllable poem best matches the traditional haiku form in English.

This collection has attempted to keep within the traditional ten to fifteen syllable form. However, the most important factor in any haiku poem is the clearness of the image a poet is attempting to portray in the haiku.

Japanese haiku is most associated with creating some type of image related to nature and the seasons. Consequently, there are poets who feel any true haiku must relate in some way to nature. However, there are also poets who view haiku as a method to portray more clearly all aspects of life. Indeed, some believe all parts of life relate to nature in some way. The author believes in the latter.

The beauty of haiku is that it is a form of poetry which projects a Zen like quality. It forces one to use their imagination to actually see an image of life that the poet is attempting to show. Unlike some forms of poetry, which sometimes has a tendency to ramble on endlessly with no purpose, the focus in a haiku poem is to provide a clear picture of life. Haiku provides a split second glance at a moment in time. The haiku poet, with just a few words, projects a slice of life, that with just a little imagination, can become a common experience of humankind.

HOW TO READ, WRITE AND UNDERSTAND HAIKU

Most masters of haiku suggest, that to better understand the feeling and image the poet is trying to covey, the reader should first read the poem, and than close their eyes. They should try to see and feel the image of the poem. The reader can than move on to the next haiku. Not all haiku will have the same impact on the reader. If one cannot relate to a particular haiku, than move on to the next one. In this way the relationship between writer and reader can form a bond by sharing a short frame of life together.

GENERAL OUTINE FOR WRITING HAIKU

It important to note that there is often disagreement among haiku experts as to specific hard rules; nevertheless, there are certain general principles that can be followed in creating haiku.

1. In general, English written haiku should follow a 10 to 17 syllable form, with the first and third lines being shorter than the second line. However, most haiku experts emphasize the importance of image creation rather than just counting syllables. Nevertheless, one should try and follow correct haiku form.

2. Haiku is a form of poetry that should focus on every day life and experiences. In this respect, haiku should reflect reality in its purest form.

3. In traditional haiku the emphasis is often on seasons and nature, but western writers of haiku have sometimes modified this general guide.

4. Use common language to simplify and clarify the poem.

5. Rhyme should be avoided in haiku, as it can defeat the purpose of the haiku poem form.

6. The image in haiku should be clear with no attempt to create obscure allusions, which unfortunately is much too common in other forms of poetry. Simple language should be used to project the image readers can see and feel.

7. Humor has been a tradition with haiku, as some of Basho's poems have demonstrated. This does not mean every haiku must have humor, but the use of it is acceptable.

8. Reading haiku properly requires a pause and reflection, in order to see and feel the image. When writing haiku, one should be moved by the specific slice of life experienced creating the haiku poem.

CONCLUSION

There are those who feel one must be Japanese to really understand and write haiku, but there are others who believe haiku is for everyone. It is true, however, that to better appreciate haiku, one should find out something about the Japanese cultural traditions.

The philosophical influences, which play such a big part in how the Japanese view life, is an area that must be considered, in order to understand the images and experiences in reading their poetry. The violent history of Japan is not unlike the experiences of most countries, including the United States.
However, even among the warring shoguns, an appreciation of poetry and other things cultural played a vital role in their historical development.

The Japanese Samurai were guided by their own code of values, based primarily on the Zen philosophy. The code of bushido emphasized that a true warrior must not only be skilled in the combat systems, but also the cultural arts. Indeed, the samurai was expected to be a person of culture as well as a warrior. One side note should be mentioned. In spite of what some people believe, there were women, who were also samurai warriors during the Genji period in Japan.

Many samurai were known for their poetry, as well as their fighting ability. This philosophy of believing in the development of the total person, in combination with being in tune with nature, is the heart and soul of Japan. This is why to fully appreciate and understand haiku, one should delve deeper into the cultural factors of those who created the haiku form.

It is sincerely hoped this modest collection of haiku will spark in interest in not only haiku, but in other Asian poetic forms. We have much to learn from their observations and sense of life.

HAIKU POEM SECTION

THE SEASONS

LAW ENFORCEMENT

TRIBUTE TO WARRIORS

THE SEASONS

SPRING FEVER

Melting snow
days growing longer
winters death near

Warm breezes
new life begins
birds singing

Green grass
starting to come alive
bare foot in park

Chirping birds
morning ritual for food
flying about

Morning sun
Leaves turning green
beginning spring

Joseph J. Truncale

Squirrels are out
running up green trees
play time

Robins are seen
making their new nests
flying for food

Light jackets
replace winter coats
spring smell in air

SUMMER HEAT

Thieves with masks
inside the garbage can
raccoons run

Speeding cars
all night long on streets
man can't sleep

People outside
so crowded and hot
blood on street

Groups of youths
roaming streets at night
vandals on prowl

Shots fired
common summer fun
youth has a gun

Joseph J. Truncale

Window broke
B-B holes in glass
parents surprised

Sirens scream
summer heats up the night
crime all around

FALL DELIGHT COLLECTION

Red leaves falling
gold leaves falling
floating angels

Children playing
On high leaf piles
youth laughing

Sweat shirts worn
chill lights the night
feel more alive

Burning leaves
smoke and haze in air
smells of fall

Football playing
watching television
man relaxing

Joseph J. Truncale

Crisp and cool
breathing in life's joy
falls reward

Frosted morning
glaze on grassy knoll
sings of fall

Goblins lurking
at your doorway
Halloween night

Bursting colors
an artist's dream
fall trees

Run and catch
football season is here
joy in motion

SEASON OF THE WARRIOR
A POETIC TRIBUTE TO WARRIORS

Brown and gold
falls yellow brick road
nature's own OZ

Squirrel running
storing precious food
falls end near

Woods bright
colors sparkle on trees
paradise on earth

Bags of leaves
falls payment for beauty
breathing clean air

Holding hands
walking in the woods
falling leaves

WINTER SEASON COLLECTION

White powder
falling in the moonlight
beautiful blanket

Silent snow
deep inside woods
mysterious calm

High snow
children playing
laughing faces

Snow mist
something hiding between trees
A deer family

Skiers ahead
tracks in new snow
sliding sound

SEASON OF THE WARRIOR
A POETIC TRIBUTE TO WARRIORS

Animal tracks
prints on fallen snow
distant deer

Snow tiger
regal and dangerous
viewed from afar

Snow flying
children in heavy coats
snow balls thrown

Music playing
sounds of the season
holiday cheer

A running brook
on snow covered ground
peaceful sound

Joseph J. Truncale

Frosted windows
Children peeking out
Santa appears

Bells ringing
a horse carries group
hoot prints in snow

Stores crowded
people buying gifts
necklace brought

Snow man starring
at children playing
as flakes fall

Lovers kiss
cold air but warm lips
hearts on fire

Sips of cider
cold winds howl outside
snuggled together

LAW ENFORCEMENT HAIKU COLLECTION

DAY BEAT COLLECTION

Armed robbery
knights with guns respond
false alarm

Dogs running
owners are not around
police look-dogs gone

Rushing cars
radar gun clocks speeders
tickets given

Fire alarm
red engines racing to scene
house ablaze

Theft from car
radar detector stolen
can't speed today

Car tracks
on the fresh mowed lawn
home owner shakes head

Runaway youth
hates school and drinks
parents on drugs

Female thief
steals purse from cart
gets caught in act

Loud noise complaint
ignorant youth with boombox
sweet silence

Joseph J. Truncale

Senile old man
confused and afraid
family located

Cars crashing
slick roads and speeding cars
a woman moans

Storm clouds above
lightening strikes a tree
fire and smoke

Drunk teenager
wandering in a daze
parents blind to truth

Black eyes
crying woman tells story
boyfriend laughs

NIGHT BEAT

(3-11 SHIFT)

Roll call
knights wearing guns
modern dragon slayers

Burglar alarm
rings loudly outside
thieves running away

Strange person
citizens call the police
salesman walks alone

A woman falls
she cries for help
firemen transport

Shopping in a fog
her purse in the cart
It is now gone

Joseph J. Truncale

Bike unlocked
youth in the store
thief rides away

Woman grabbed
a man with a knife
she shoots attacker

Glass shatters
vandals throwing rocks
window broken

Traffic jam
broken down car on street
tow truck takes away

Protest group walk
carry message signs
people just ignore

SEASON OF THE WARRIOR
A POETIC TRIBUTE TO WARRIORS

A child cries
parents fighting
custody battle

Youth with gun
shoots from moving car
someone dies

Flashing blade
a throat is cut
a man screams

Drunken mother
hanging out in a bar
children are alone

Shot gun on floor
red all over walls
head is gone

Joseph J. Truncale

GRAVE YARD SHIFT COLLECTION

Night screams
sirens mournful tune
dead body on ground

Cars crashing
people on the ground
ambulance coming

Explosion
youths run away fast
mailbox blown up

Train bearing down
woman walking on tracks
parents mourn

Couple fighting
police calm them down
they kiss-make up

SEASON OF THE WARRIOR
A POETIC TRIBUTE TO WARRIORS

drunks at a bar
beer bottles fly about
two fools arrested

Shots fired
bloody bodies in sight
police arrive

Arrive home
burglars broke in house
jewelry is gone

A baby cries
bruises and burn marks
police take baby away

Midnight beat
speeding car squeals tires
on a quiet street

Joseph J. Truncale

Motel calls
drunks trashing room
police arrest group

TRIBUTE TO WARRIORS HAIKU COLLECTION

Flashing swords
Two men clash in battle
Spartans play

Breathing fire
dragon showing his power
knight with sword

Centurions
preparing for battle
Rome's pride

Samurai code
ready to fight enemies
calm warrior

Cheering crowds
men with weapons in hand
gladiators salute

Joseph J. Truncale

Smoky ring
gloved warriors fighting
boxers punching

Muscular bodies
attempting to pin
wrestlers grapple

Thailand pride
ring music playing
Muay-thai Warriors

Reverse punch
woman in white GI
ippon scored

High kicks
thrown at same time
Tai Kwon Do play

Foot trip
two men grapple
Judo players

Calmness of mind
attackers fly about
Zen in motion

Wrist throw
attackers hit the mat
Gentle art

Gun on hips
knights in squad cars
fighting crime

Silver shield
dead officer honored
officer salute

Joseph J. Truncale

Men in black
swimming toward danger
SEALS in action

First to fight
a few good men needed
Marines call

Many try
few are chosen
Green Berets

Flying high
warriors in the air
fighter pilots

Covered faces
black uniform in dark
Ninja way

SEASON OF THE WARRIOR
A POETIC TRIBUTE TO WARRIORS

Trapping hands
close inside fighting
Wing Chun woman

Bamboo swords clash
slidding feet across floor
Kendo warriors

Taking aim
knife at woman's throat
SWAT member fires

Small town
western sheriff walks
draws and fires gun

Women in motion
sticks in their hands
Arnis players

Big men clashing
Sumo wrestlers fighting
Japan's pride

Clashing sticks
Quick and deadly
Hanbo practice

ESSAYS ON THE WAY OF THE WARRIOR

The following essays were written for two newsletters I have written and published over the last eight years. One was the Street Warrior, which focused on law enforcement issues and the other was The Samurai Heart, which I still publish bi-monthly for my martial art students. These essays deal with several warrior philosophy issues. They will be of interest to anyone attempting to understand what the way of the warrior is as it relates to modern society. These have been edited for this book, but they are the same essays that were originally published in my newsletters.

The following essays include:

* Where Are All The Warriors

* What Is Honor To The Warrior

* What Is The Warrior's Heart

WHERE ARE ALL THE WARRIORS?

May be I am too idealistic when it comes to the qualities I think police officers should have in our society. I've talked with many police officers and trainers across the country about the lack of a warrior spirit among many police officers and police trainers today. One police instructor told me of his experience. He was teaching a class of officers control techniques using the PR-24 police baton. One of the students came up to him complaining about having to practice the control holds because they were painful. Another instructor was teaching handcuffing techniques when a supervisor asked if they could just pretend to handcuff each other because the handcuffs hurt their wrists. Finally, one instructor received a phone call from a supervisor who wanted to send one of his officers to an O.C. (pepper) Spray instructor certification course, but the officer did not want to be sprayed. The OC instructor explained why it was important for officers, especially those who aspire to become instructors, to experience first hand how it feels to be sprayed with OC spray. This supervisor gave some irrational excuses, which we have all heard before on this issue, and he refused to change his view on the subject. He never did send an officer to the instructor class. One police instructor calls this "the whimp factor." However, there is a deeper philosophical and psychological problem that needs to be addressed. What seems to be missing is this simple truth and fact, THAT NOTHING OF REAL VALUE CAN BE ACHIEVED WITHOUT SOME PAIN AND DISCOMFORT. True warriors understand that to survive in the world requires one to experience life in its entirety. This includes the good, the bad and the ugly. The pleasurable and the painful. If officers are to survive and win on the street, they need to experience some pain and discomfort in their training. The old warrior saying holds true even today. "The more you sweat in training the less you bleed on the street." We need to begin teaching the warrior philosophy in all our training courses. To answer the question, "Where are all the warriors? They are still around, but unfortunately, it seems in fewer and fewer numbers.

****

WHAT IS HONOR TO THE WARRIOR?

It is important to review and understand this vital quality of "honor" as it relates to the "Code of Bushido." Because a true warrior is usually stronger, more educated, and more powerful than most of the non-warrior individuals within a society, there is a heavy burden of responsibility to assume the role of protector in a society. This means you must apply the quality of honor to your own life. As a warrior you must act with honor and not just talk about it. Some of the attributes of honor include the following:

1. TRUTHFULNESS: The samurai understood that being truthful was essential to real courage. It meant taking responsibility for your actions and facing up to your obligations. The Samurai believed that the person who lies is not just dishonest, but also is a coward. To the Samurai, being truthful relates directly to having courage.
2. COURTESY: Sadly, it often seems that being polite is a forgotten art in our modern society. Those who follow the way of the warrior realize that courtesy is an essential quality in all dealings with others within a society. You will often notice in a traditional martial arts club, that the most humble and courteous people in the school are usually the most senior.
3. RESTRAINT: You may have heard the term: "The Sword that takes life is the same sword that gives life."

The warrior, being more powerful and stronger than non-warriors in a society has the obligation to never abuse his or her power. In ancient Japan it was the Samurai who served the role of protector. He used restraint in most cases, involving non-warriors. In our modern society, the police have the power to kill, but cannot use that power unless there is no other option available. There must be a chance of great bodily harm or death involved before an officer can employ deadly force. This is the kind of restraint warriors must adhere to within a civilized society.

4. LOYALTY: When a society does not value loyalty, the result is always treachery. The warrior realizes that in order to function with true honor, there must be loyalty to both superiors and subordinates in a society or group. In the martial arts those who are loyal to their teachers share a bond. Indeed, teachers must also show loyalty. It is the YIN and YANG of the teacher and student relationship.
5. SERVICE: I have mentioned several times in the past the importance of GIRI to the true warrior. This term refers to paying back something to society for the knowledge you have gained from practicing the way of the warrior. This can include many things such as offering free self defense classes to seniors, and giving free assault prevention seminars to women.

****

WHAT IS THE WARRIOR'S HEART? (OR THE ART OF WINNING, AND NOT JUST SURVIVING).

We in the martial arts often speak of such things as "The Code of Bushido." Indeed, most of use try to live by the warrior philosophy. However, in spite of our training, we may not really know whether we truly have a warrior's heart until a situation forces us to do things we never thought were possible.

Fortunately, we have many examples of those who showed courage under the most stressful of times. The fire fighters and police officers in New York on 09-11-2001 is an example of what the warrior heart really means. There were thousands of stories of courage in action during that tragic time in our history.

It is not just in a national crisis that the warrior heart is seen. Two police incidents that have been widely reported in law enforcement circles but are not so well known to the public can serve as examples of NOT JUST SURVIVING BUT OF WINNING. This is an essential trait of a warrior.

THE OFFICER JOHN WILBUR INCIDENT: This vehicle stop from hell began when officer wilbur came upon a suspicious car with three occupants. When Officer Wilbur looked inside the car he saw three subjects who appeared to be sleeping. However, what was suspicious is that it was a very warm evening and the three subjects were wearing gloves. When officer Wilbur walked up to the car the occupants began to stir. At this point one of the subjects in the back seat took something from his lap (drugs) and immediately put it in his mouth. Officer Wilbur opened up the back door and told the subject to spit out what was in his mouth.

At this time a struggle began and the subject closed the back door on officer Wilbur's left hand. The officer's wedding ring caught in the door when the car took off, dragging officer Wilbur with it. At speeds of over 70 MPH, officer Wilbur somehow managed to draw his gun out and fire into the back window, striking two of the three subjects. The officer was thrown from the car, causing numerous serious injuries to his feet, legs and buttocks. The officer had to spend several months in the hospital and somehow survived. This is not all the stress this poor officer endured. Even though the officer was in every way within his rights to save his own life, there were special interest groups who tried to get him indicted. There is a short 15 minute video out on this incident put out by Calibre Press.

The lessons learned from this incident include:

1. You can survive damn near anything.
2. Body armor is important.
3. Never commit your body inside a vehicle.
4. Accept that gunfights can occur in unusual cases.
5. When you've done the right thing, believe in yourself.

THE STACY LIM SHOOTING: A GIANT AMONG WARRIORS."

One night, off duty, and alone after some softball practice, officer Stacy Lim returned home. Exiting her vehicle in the dirveway, she was surprised by a group of gang-bangers. They had followed her home with the motive of car-jacking. Stacy Lim's fight begins when she is shot in the chest with a .357 magnum, which causes a tennis ball size exit wound out her back. Among the damage caused, is the bullet penetrating her heart.

Stacy Lim's custom was to have a pistol in her hand from her vehicle to her home. She lived in a high crime neighborhood. In this instance, her response to the surprise "man with a gun stimulus" was to first shout "Police Officer" as a warning. This was when she was shot in the heart. Stacy Lim stayed in the fight, not only returning fire, but became the aggressor. She never gave up, pursuing the retreating gang-banger, and hitting him with all four of the rounds she fired. The remaining gang-bangers fled when faced with the aggression of a real warrior.

Both combatants died. Stacy Lim died twice on the operating table. Eight months later, Stacy returned to duty after earning a winning survival award. Today, she works in uniform patrol on the streets of Los Angeles. Here are some lessons learned.

Stacy Lim was both physically and mentally prepared. She had a competive attitude that refused to lose. Stacy had a plan and visualized with determination, always winning. Stacy Lim was a victim of a surprise attack by predatory gang-bangers, but she stayed in the fight and was victorious.

These two examples can serve as guide to what it means to have the heart of a warrior.

CONCLUSION

It is sincerely hoped you have enjoyed this poetic tribute to warriors, and better understand the heart and soul of those who have chosen to follow the demanding path of the warrior. I think it is appropriate to end this tribute with this final poem.

IF

If I were a tree so strong, with leaves forever grown.
If I were a field so green, how beautiful the land.
If I were an ocean so deep, my waves would kiss the shore.
If I were a floating cloud, to be calm and serene.
If I were a flower so sweet, perfume would fill the air.
If I were a plant to grow, giving life to nature.
If I were a tiger so quick, to leap high in joy.
If I were a warrior so brave, bringing freedom and peace to all.
If I were to live forever, immortality would be mine.
If I were always healthy and strong, to always move forward.
If I were always young, old age would never be.
If I were a poet, whose words inspire beauty and love.
If I were a doctor, to cure all illness in the world.
If I were a rich man, to help people help themselves.
If I were a scientist, to bring progress to humankind.

If I were an artist, painting the world a picture.
If I were an astronaut, to explore the heavens above.
If I were an archaeologist, searching for meaning in the past.

But in reality, I am only a simple human searching for himself.

Joseph J. Truncale

BOOKS, MANUALS, GUIDES&VIDEOS BY JOSEPH J. TRUNCALE

1. PR-24 Baton Techniques: Basic and Advanced: PUB. Univ. of Ill Press (Co-Author)
2. Police Yawara Stick Techniques: PUB. Univ. of Ill Press (Co-Author)
3. Advanced PR-24 Baton Techniques: PUB by Monadnock Prod. Inc.
4. Use of The Monadnock Straight Baton: PUB. by Monadnock Prod. Inc.
5. The Monadnock Defensive Tactics System Manual: Monadnock: (Co-Author)
6. The Persuader Baton: (Revised original text written by Eric Chambers) Monadnock.
7. Mechanics of Arrest and Control: PUB. Rational Press
8. The Rational Approach to Arrest and Control: PUB. Rational Press
9. Persuader Defense Systems Manual: PUB. Pro-Systems
10. Basic Handbook of Hypnosis for Law Enforcement: PUB. Pro-Systems
11. Rational Self Hypnosis for Police Officers: PUB. Pro-Systems
12. Rational Self Hypnosis for Everyone: PUB. Pro-Systems
13. Use of The Key Chain Holder For Self Defense: (Co-author)
14. The Pro-Systems Official Weapon Retention Manual.

15. The Pro-Systems Use of Pepper Spray for Self Defense Course Manual.
16. The FIST (Fast-Intense-Strong-Techniques) System of Self Defense.
17. A Quick Course Guide to Women's Self Defense: (Pro-Systems)
18. A Quick Course Guide to the Use of The Persuader Baton: (Pro-Systems)
19. A Quick Course Guide to Total Physical Fitness: (Pro-Systems)
20. A Quick Course Guide to the Use of The Scientific Method & Pseudoscience.
21. A Quick Course Guide to Writing For Publication: (Pro-Systems)
22. A Quick Course Guide to Great Books of Civilization: (Pro-Systems)
23. A Quick Course Guide to Elements in Officer Survival: (Pro-Systems)
24. Facts and Fallacies in Police Defensive Tactics Manual: (Pro-Systems)
25. Truth and Fiction in the Martial Arts and Self Defense Manual: (Pro-Systems)
26. Common Myths About Women's Self Defense: (Pro-Systems)
27. A Basic Guide to Defending Against Chokes Manual: (Pro-Systems)
28. Season Of The Warrior: A Poetic Tribute To Warriors: Poems and Essay Collection: (Pro-Systems)
29. A Tribute To Warriors: A Haiku Collection: (Pro-Systems)

30. Nothing Ever Happens In Glenview Poem Collection:(Pro-Systems)
31. The Bushi Satori Ryu Official Student and Instructor Manual.
32. The Bushi Satori Ryu Official 15 Weapons Basic Manual.
33. Knife Handling and Knife Defense For Law Enforcement Manual: (Pro-Systems)
34. Use of The Knife for Women's Self Defense: A Basic Manual: (Pro-Systems)
35. Samurai Aerobics Manual: The Bushi Satori Ryu Official Kenjutsu/Iaijutsu manual for students and instructors: (Pro-Systems & Bushi Satori Ryu)
36. Basic Use of the Cane Summary Review Paper: (Bushi Satori Ryu)
37. Basic Use of the Cane Manual: (Bushi Satori Ryu)
38. The Pro-Systems and Bushi Satori Ryu 3-4 and 6-4 Knife Course Outline.
39. The Pro-Systems and Bushi Satori Ryu 3-4 and 6-4 Knife System Official Manual.
40. Revised 12-4 Knife Combat System of Bushi Satori Ryu.

****

PRO-SYSTEMS/BUSHI SATORI RYU SUMMARY REVIEW VIDEOS (NOTE: THESE ARE NOT INSTRUCTIONAL VIDEOS BUT WERE DESIGNED ONLY FOR THOSE STUDENTS SEEKING A REVIEW OF THE COURSE MATERIAL THAT THEY HAVE TAKEN)

1. BASIC USE OF THE CANE SUMMARY REVIEW VIDEO

2. BASIC KNIFE HANDLING AND DEFENSE REVIEW VIDEO

3. BASIC PR-24 COURSE OVERVIEW VIDEO

4. BASIC MEB (MONADNOCK EXP/STRAIGHT BATON) COURSE REVIEW OUTLINE VIDEO.

5. BASIC MDTS (Monadnock Defensive Tactics System) REVIEW OUTLINE VIDEO.

6. BASIC CLAMP COURSE OVERVIEW VIDEO.

7. BASIC WEAPON RETENTION COURSE OVERVIEW VIDEO.

8. SAMURAI AEROBICS WORKOUT TAPE TAKEN DURING ONE CLASS.

NOTE: THERE ARE NUMEROUS SUMMARY REVIEW VIDEOS THAT ARE IN THE PLANNING STAGES OF BEING DEVELOPED SOMETIME IN THE FUTURE: These Include the the following: Basic GRASP Course overview, Bushi Satori Ryu Warm Up Kata, The First 27 two person Katas of Bushi Satori Ryu, The Ten No Kata of Bushi Satori Ryu, The Zen In Motion Kata of Bushi Satori Ryu, Basic Katana Cuts (Kenjutsu) of Bushi Satori Ryu, The Hojo Kata of Kashima Shinden Jinkinshin Kage Ryu, and Basic Shotokan Karate Techniques of Bushi Satori Ryu.

SPECIAL THANKS AND ACKNOWLEDGMENTS

One of the special qualities that all true martial art masters have is their loyalty and appreciation to those who have trained them. One does not forget or disregard the source of any original knowledge. This acknowledgment of those masters who have come before us is an honored tradition in all Ryus (schools) in Japan, as well as other Asian martial art schools and systems. They all record the history of their particular art and previous masters of their school(s). I have been fortunate to have studied with some of the finest martial artists in the world, and this is my small way of giving thanks for what all of them have taught me. In all honesty, I have learned things from so many talented instructors, both personally as well as through their books and videos, that I could never hope to remember all their names. For example, I cannot recall the names of the two Japanese Judo instructors I trained under when I was stationed in Japan while in the U.S. Navy in 1961-1962. I trained with them at the base gym every time I was in port off duty. If I have forgotten anyone, please forgive me. However, I thank all of you for the knowledge you have given me in the Budo arts, police tactics, and most of all for your philosophical guidance.

Joseph J. Truncale

Lon Anderson: Master PR-24 Baton Instructor who was my mentor in the PR-24 Baton.

Paul Starrett: A good friend of law enforcement and a person who has my loyalty.

Terry Smith: A good friend, police trainer and fellow warrior of the street.

Larry Smith: One of my best friends, who shared his Aikido techniques, as well as so many other educational things. A fellow martial artist and warrior.

Ed. Nowicki: One of my best friends, who taught me how to be a more effective police instructor, and who along with Terry Smith, Larry Smith and Paul Starrett have my loyalty and friendship.

Terry Campbell: A good friend and fellow police trainer who stressed finishing a technique.

Mr. S. Sugiyama, Sensei: My first Karate Instructor in the United States, who tested and promoted me to Shodan (1st degree) in 1973.

Mr. Copeland: One of my first Karate Instructors (around 1968).

Mr. Loren Rogers: He helped develop my Karate skills at his Des Plaines Club.

Pro. Thomas Burdine-Soke: Kokon Ryu Bujutsu Renmei: A master of Aikido and many other arts, who taught me much whenever we got together.

Arthur (Hap) & Jan Wittkamp: Judo / Jujitsu masters, who are good friends, who helped me improve my Judo skills and achieve rank in Judo. We happily teach together at the Des Plaines YMCA.

Yutora Judo Club: I taught the practical self defense class for them and the black belts helped me improve my Judo.

Brian Smith: A Hakkoryu Jujitsu expert and friend who shared his techniques with me.

Dennis G. Palumbo: A Hakkoryu Jujitsu Master who shared his system with me.

Tak Kubota: A Karate Master who trained me in his Kubotan techniques in 1980. Rorian, Hoyce and Rickson Gracie: Who I had the honor of training under at several seminars in Chicago.

Kyung Sun Shin: A Judo master who shared his Judo and TaeKwondo Techniques with me.

Mr. Choi: Who further developed my TaeKwondo techniques when he was in the U.S.

Jim Marsh: Who taught me his "Speed Cuffing" techniques with me at seminars.

Tim & Mike Lynch: Both of them shared their vast martial arts knowledge with me.

Wally Jay: The founder of Small Circle Jujitsu, who is a true master and gentleman, and who I was honored to have learned from personally at two seminars.

Remy Presas: The founder of Modern Arnis, who is also a true master and gentleman. I had the honor to train under him at several seminars.

Leo Gaje, Jr: A master of Arnis and Knife techniques I was honored to learn from at several police instructor seminars.

Gary Klugawicz: The founder of "Active Counter Measures" I trained under.

James Lindell: The founder of the Lindell Weapon Retention and Neck Restraint systems, and who I was honored to have known and trained under.

Massad Ayoob: A friend of mine and law enforcement, who is a well known gun expert.

Robert Lindsey: A friend, fellow police trainer and a life time student of the Budo Arts.

Sean Curtin & Two Ex-Pro-Boxers who taught my son and I the finer points of John Lera: American Boxing. There was no slack time in their gym.

John Vasquez: A old friend who shared his Police Nunchaku techniques with me, and my sparring partner at the week long Krave Mage Instructor Class.

George Sylvain: An old friend and the inventor of the Scepter Baton.

Phillip Messina: A friend who heads the Modern Warrior Training institute.

Guy Rossi: A friend, who always asked the question–"But can he fight?" Dennis Juaraz: A friend and fellow police trainer who shared a lot of laughs with me.

Arthur Cohen: A friend who shared his ground fighting techniques with me.

Tim Powers: For sharing his "Tactical Aerobics" with me.

Dr. Kenneth Cooper: I was honored to have met him when I attended and graduated from his Institute for Aerobic Research week long course.

Dr. Kenneth Miller: My instructor in Kashima-Shinden-Jikinshin Kage Ryu Kenjutsu Stye.

Chicago Kendo Club: Great people who taught me the basics of Kendo.

Both of the above were held at the Japanese Culture Center in Chicago.

Phillip Porter, O'Sensei: Former President of the U.S. Judo Association and now is the President of the United States Martial Arts Association(USMA). I am proud to have been awarded my Judo and Jujitsu Black Belt certificates from him. A true Master and gentleman.

Antonio Pereira: The founder of Miyama Ryu Jujitsu: A great Jujitsu style.

D'Arcy Rahming: A gentleman and author of Combat Jujitsu and Advanced Combat Jujitsu: He used to have a Miyama Ryu Jujitsu club in Chicago.

Shoto Tanemura: Grandmaster of Kokusai Jujitsu Renmei, whose skills in the ancient arts are clearly demonstrated in his videos. They are excellent.

Kyoshi Masayuki Shimabukuro: A master of Eishin-Ryu Iaido. His video series and book are the best information on the Eishin Ryu System.
Very informative material.

Helen Nakano: She is one of the co-founders of the U.S. Naginata Federation and has two excellent and beautiful videos on the use of the Naginata.

Kensho Furuya: His philosophical insights into the ancient Budo Arts are truly enlightening and inspiring. His book Kodo: Ancient Ways, should be read and studied by every martial artist and warrior.

TO ALL THOSE WHO HAVE SHARED ONE TECHNIQUE OR TEN THOUSAND TECHNIQUES WITH ME, AND TO ALL MY STUDENTS, PAST, PRESENT AND FUTURE, I SINCERELY ACKNOWLEDGE AND THANK ALL OF YOU FROM THE BOTTOM OF MY HEART.

Joseph J. Truncale, Kudan (Soke) Founder: Bushi Satori Ryu (Warrior Enlightenment School)

SELECTED REFERENCES, AND RECOMMENDED BOOKS & VIDEOS IN MY

PERSONAL LIBRARY

My insatiable thirst for more knowledge, in both the Martial arts and other fields, has been a joyous lifetime pursuit. This has led me to study and learn from numerous people. I learned from their books, videos, as well as in person whenever possible. The following is a list, though certainly not complete, as I have an extensive martial arts library, of the many books and videos I have studied over the years. The list, however, can serve as a basic guide to increase your own martial art and self defense knowledge. Many of these books are classics and may be out of print.

1. Albert, Frank.: One Strike Stopping Power. Paladin Press
2. Applegate, Rex Col.: Combat Use of the Double-Edged Fighting Knife. Paladin Press.
3. Applegate, Rex Col.: Kill or Get KIlled. (A Classic) Paladin Press
4. Applegate, Rex Col.: The Close Combat Files of Col. Rex Applegate. Paladin Press.
5. Ayoob, Massad.: In The Gravest Extreme. Lethal Force Institute.
6. Ayoob, Massad.: The Ayoob Files: The Book. Paladin Press.
7. Ayoob, Massad.: The Truth About Self Protection.

8. Beasley, Jerry.: The Jeet Kune Do Experience. Paladin Press.
9. Beaumont, Ned.: Championship Streetfighting: Boxing as a Marial art. Paladin.
10. Beaumont, Ned.: The Savage Science of Streetfighting. Paladin Press.
11. Beaver, William,: Practical Martial Arts For Special Forces, Paladin Press.
12. Benson, Ragnar.: Switchblade: The Ace of Blades. Paladin Press.
13. Campbell, Sid.: Kobudo and Bugei. Paladen Press.
14. Cassidy, William.: The Complete Book of Knife Fighting. Paladin Press.
15. Christensen, Loren.: The Fighter's Fact Book. Paladin Press.
16. Christensen, Loren.: Fighting Power. Paladin Press.
17. Christensen, Loren.: The Way Alone: Your Path to Excellence. Paladin Press.
18. Cirillo, Jim.: Guns, Bullets, and Gun Fights. Paladin Press
19. Cohen, Arthur.: Street Wise: A Woman's Guide to Self Protection. Target.
20. Cosneck, B.J.: American Combat Judo. (May be out of print.)
21. Daniel, Charles.: Kenjutsu: The Art of Japanese Swordmanship. Unique Pub.
22. Daniel, Charles.: Ninja Weapons. Unique Pub.
23. Demura, Fumio.: Shito-Ryu Karate. Ohara is pubisher for all Demura's books.

24. Demura, Fumio.: Nunchaku, Advanced Nunchaku, Bo, Sai, Kama, Bo Books.

25. DePasquale Jr. Michael: Guide to Jujitsu. Monarch Press Pub.

26. Draeger & Smith.: Asian Fighting Arts (A classic for all martial artists) Kodansha

27. Draeger, Donn F.: Classical Bujutsu 3 VOLS-SET. 1, 2, 3,... Weatherhill Pub.

28. Echanis, Michael.: Knife Defense For Combat. Ohara Pub.

29. Echanis, Michael.: Knife Fighting, Knife Throwing for Combat. Ohara Pub.

30. Echanis, Michael.: Stick Fighting For Combat. Ohara Pub.

31. Finn, Michael.: Iaido: The Way of the Sword. Crompton Pub.

32. Franco, Sammy.: Street Lethal: Unarmed Urban Combat. Paladin Press.

33. Franco, Sammy.: The Bigger They Are, The Harder They Fall. Paladin Press.

34. Funakoshi, Gichen.: Karate Do: Kyohan. Kodansha International Pub.

35. Funakoshi, Gichen.: Karate Do: My Way of Life. Kodansha International.

36. Funakoshi, Gichen.: Karate-Do Nyumon. Kodansha International.

37. Gambordella, Ted.: The 100 Deadliest Karate Moves. Paladin Press

38. Gambordella, Ted.: The Complete Book of Martial Art Weapons. Paladin Press.

39. Gilbey, John F.: Secret Fighting Arts of The World. Charles C. Tuttle
40. Gluck, Jay.: Zen Combat. (A classic) Weatherhill Pub.
41. Gruzanski, Charles.: Spike and Chain: Japanese Fighting Arts. Tuttle Co. A Classic.
42. Hancock & Higashi.: The Complete Kano Jiu-jitsu(Judo) Dover Pub. A Classic.
43. Hartsell, Larry.: Jeet Kune Do: Entering to Trapping Vo. 1, 2. Unique Pub.
44. Hatsumi, Massaki& Stick Fighting: Techniques of Self Defense. Kodansha. Chambers, Quintin.:
45. Hays, Stephen K.: His entire Ninja series books are fantastic. Ohara Pub.
46. Holifield, Leonard.: Close-Quarter Combat: A Soldier's Guide. Paladin Press.
47. Imada, Jeff.: The Balisong Manual. Know Now Pub.
48. Imada, Jeff.: The Advanced Balisong Manual. Know Now Pub.
49. Inosanto, Dan.: The Filipino Martial Arts. Know Now Pub.
50. Inosanto, Dan.: Absorb What is Useful(Jeet Kune Do) Know Now Pub.
51. Janich, Michael.: Knife Fighting: A Practical Course. Paladin Press Pub.
52. Jay, Wally.: Small Circle Jujitsu. Ohara Pub.
53. Jenks, & Brown.: Prison's Bloody Iron. Paladin Press Pub.
54. Jones, Jan.: Self Defense Requires No Apology. Security World Pub.

55. Kary, & Nardi.: American Combatives: Military Combat. Koinonia Prod.
56. Kaufman, Stephen.: Zen and The Art of Stick Fighting. Contemporary Books.
57. Kent & Tackett.: Jeet Kune Do Kickboxing Techniques. Unique Pub.
58. Kirby, George.: Jujitsu: The Gentle Art. Volumes 1 and 2. Ohara Pub.
59. KIrby, George.: Jutte: Japanese Power of Ten Hands. Ohara Pub.
60. Kubota, Takayuki.: Close Encounters: Art of Taiho-Jitsu Dragon Books
61. Kubota, Takayuki.: Fighting Karate: Gosoku Style. Unique Pub.
62. Kubota, Takayuki.: Kubotan: Weapon of Attitude Adjustement. Unique Pub.
63. LaFond, James.: The Logic of Steel. Paladin Press Pub.
64. LaTourrette, John.: Mental Training of a Warrior. Sport Psychology Inst.
65. LaTourrette, John.: Warrior's Guide to Knife fighting. Paladin Press.
66. LeBell, Gene.: Grappling Master: Combat for Street Defense. Pro-Action
67. LeBell, Gene.: Grappling World: Encyclopedia of Holds. Pro-Action Pub.
68. LeBell, Gene.: Handbook of Judo. Pro-Action pub.
69. LeBell, Gene.: Handbook of Self Defense. Pro-Action Pub.
70. LeBell, Gene.: Club Master: Grappling with a club. Pro-Action Pub.

71. Lee, Bruce.: Tao of Jeet Kune Do. (A classic by Lee) Ohara Pub.
72. Lee, Bruce.: Skill in Techniques. Ohara Pub.
73. Lee, Bruce.: Advanced Techniques. Ohara Pub.
74. Lee, Bruce.: Self Defense Techniques. Ohara Pub.
75. Lee Joo Bang.: The Ancient Martial Art of Hwarang Do. (series) Ohara Pub.
76. Lowrey, Dave.: Autumn LIghtening: Education of a Samurai. Shambhala Pub.
77. Lowrey, Dave.: Sword and Brush. Shambhala Pub.
78. Lowrey, Dave.: JO: The art of the Japanese Short Staff. Ohara Pub.
79. Lowrey, Dave.: Bokken: The art of the Japanese Wooden Sword. Ohara Pub.
80. Machowicz, Richard: Unleashing The Warrior Within. Hyperion Pub.
81. MacYoung, Marc.: Knives, Knife Fighting and Related Hassles. Paladin Press.
82. MacYoung, Marc.: Pool Cues, Beer Bottles & Baseball Bats. Paladin Press.
83. MacYoung, Marc.: Taking It To The Streets. Paladin Press.
84. MacYoung, Marc.: Cheap Shots, mbushes, and other Lessons. Paladin Press.
85. Marcinko, Richard.: Leadership Secrets of the Rogue Warrior. Pocket Books Pub.
86. Mashiro, N.: Black Medicine (The Whole Series are great) Paladin Press.
87. Maynard, Russell.: Tanto: Japanese Knives and Knife Fighting. Unique Pub.

88. McKay, Robert S.: Modern American Fighting Knives. Unique Pub.

89. McSweeney, John.: Street Karate: A Complete Course in S.D. Paladin Press.

90. Mitose, James M.: What is Self Defense. A classic that could be hard to find.

91. Morgan, Forrest E.: Living The Martial Way. (A Great Book) Barricade Books Pub.

92. Mroz, Ralph.: Defensive Shooting For Real Life Encounters. Paladin Press.

93. Nakae, Kiyose.: Jujitsu Complete. Another classic that could be hard to find.

94. Nakayama, M.: Dynamic Karate and all his other books and series are great.

95. Nishiyama & Brown.: Karate: Art of Empty Hand Fighting. Tuttle Pub.

96. Nowicki, Edward.: True Blue: True Police Officer Stories. Performance Dim. Pub.

97. Nowicki & Ramsey.: Street Weapons. Performance Dimensions Pub.

98. Nowicki, Edward.: Total Survival: Advice from the Pros. Performance Dim Pub.

99. Obata, Toshishiro.: Samurai Aikijutsu. Dragon Pub.

100. Oyama, Mas.: The Kyokushin Way. Japan Pub.

101. Oyama, Mas.: What is Karate? Japan Pub.

102. Oyama, Mas.: This is Karate. Japan Pub.

103. Oyama, Mas.: Advanced Karate. Japan Pub.

104. Palumbo, Dennis G.: Hakko Ryu Jujitsu: Shodan, Nidan, Sandan. Paladin Press.

105. Parulski Jr., eorge R.: Sword of The Samurai. Paladin Press

106. Pentecost, Don.: Put Em Down, Take Em Out Knife Fighting. Paladin Press.

107. Presas, Remy.: Modern Arnis. Ohara Pub.

108. Quigley, Paxton.: Armed and Female. E.P. Dutton Pub.

109. Quinn, Peyton.: A Bouncer's Guide to Barroom Brawling. Paladin Press.

110. Quinn, Peyton.: Real Fighting. Paladin Press.

111. Rahming, D'Arcy.: Combat Jujitsu and Advanced Combat Jujitsu. (Miyama Ryu)

112. Remsberg&Adams&Mcterman.: Street Survival: Tactics for Armed Encounters.

113. Remsberg, Charles.: The Tactical Edge: Surviving High Risk Patrol. Calibre Press.

114. Remsberg, Charles.: Tactics for Criminal Patrol: Vehicle Stops Etc. Calibre Press.

115. Rice, Rodney, R.: 101 Weapons for Woman. Ri-Jo Productions. Paladin Press.

116. Ryan, Richard.: Master of The Blade. Paladin Press.

117. Sanchez, John.: Blade Master: Advanced Knife Tech. Paladin Press.

118. Shimabukuro&Pellman.: Flashing Steel: Eishin Ryu Iaido. Frog Publications.

119. Spear, Robert K.: Hapkido: The Integrated Fighting Art. Unique Pub.

120. Steiner, Bradley J.: No Second Chance: Disarming the Armed. Paladin Press.

121. Steiner, Bradley J.: Principles of personal Combat Combato Pub.

122. Stevens, John.: Three Budo Masters. Kano, Funakoshi, Ueshiba. Kodansha.

123. Styers & Schuon.: Cold Steel. Paladin Press.

124. Suino, Nicklaus.: The Art of Japanese Swordsmanship. Weatherhill Pub.

125. Tegner, Bruce.: The Complete Book of Jukado. Bantam Book.

126. Tegner, Bruce.: The Complete Book of Judo. Bantam Book.

127. Tegner, Bruce.: The Complete Book of Jujitsu. Bantam Book.

128. Tegner, Bruce.: The Complete Book of Karate. Bantam Book.

129. Tegner, Bruce.: Aikido: & Jiu-Jitsu Hold and Locks. Thor Pub.

130. Tegner, Bruce.: Stick Fighting for Self Defense. Thor Pub.

131. Tegner, Bruce.: Nerve Centers and Pressure Points. Thor Pub.

132. Tegner & McGraith.: Self Defense for Women: A Simple Method. Thor Pub.

133. Tzu, Sun (Cleary).: The Art of War (Trans. by Thomas Cleary) Shambhala Pub.

134. Urquidez, Benny.: Training and Fighting Skills. Unique Pub.

135. Urquidez, Benny.: Karate Dynamics: The Ukidokan System. Pro-Action Pub.

136. Vassolo, Michael.: Desperate Measures: Unarmed Against Weapons. Paladin.

137. Vassolo, Michael.: Kamikaze Fighting. Paladin Press.

138. Walker, Greg.: Modern Knife Combat. Paladin Press.

139. Warner & Draeger.: Japanese Swordsmanship. Weatherhill Pub.

140. Wilson, William S.: Ideals of the Samurai. Ohara Pub.

141. Wilson, William S.: Budoshoshinshu. Ohara Pub.

BASIC MARTIAL ARTS GLOSSARY

This glossary was included so those reading this book can better understand some of the Japanese terms I used in some of my poems.

You should study this glossary and become familiar with these terms in order to appreciate the way of the warrior.

Age uke: Rising Block: Used to block an attack to the head and face area.

Ai: Harmony: As used in Aikido to blend with your opponent and use their own power to defeat them.

Aikido: Way of harmony: A Japanese martial art which uses the attacker's own strength to defeat him. Founder of Aikido is Morihei Uyeshiba.

Aikijutsu: Art of spirit/harmony: The predeccsor of Aikido.

Minamoto No Yoshimitsu (1036-1127) credited with inventing Aikijutsu.

Armlock: (Udegarami) A leverage technique used to control an opponent's arm by the use of pain and leverage.

Arnis:(Arnis De Mano) A martial art developed in the Philippines, in which the focus is on the use of sticks and knives for self defense.

Ashi Barai: Foot Sweep throw in Judo and Jujitsu.

Ashi Garami: Leg entanglement, where the opponent's leg is wrapped with one's own leg to throw the opponent.

Ashi Guruma: Leg wheel, where Tori places his/her foot at the knee level of Uke to throw opponent.Judo/Jujitsu

Ashi Waza: Foot Techniques: A classification of all Judo/Jujitsu throws which use the leg or foot.

Atemi Waza: Body Striking Techniques used in Judo/Jujitsu that focus on striking vulnerable areas of the body.

Back Fist: (Uraken) A snapping punch using the back of the knuckles.

Back Kick: A kick used using the heel portion of the foot at an opponent who is behind the defender. Karate, Jujitsu and other arts imploy this kick.

Bajutsu: Art of Horsemanship.

Balisong: A Philippine style of folding knife.

Bando: A Burmese system on the art of armed and unarmed fighting.

Basho: One of the six major 15 day annual Sumo tournaments.

Basho, Matsuo (1644-1694). Person responsible for first creating the poetic form of Haiku.

Basics: The elemental techniques of which all martial arts are built.

Bassi: A karate kata meaning "to penetrate a fortress."

Batto-jutsu: The art of drawing and cutting with the sword. Now referred to, in most cases, as Iaido or Iaijutsu.

Belt: A cloth fabric worn around the waist. Japanese term for belt is Obi.

Black Belt: Sign of achievement that means student has mastered the basics of a particular martial art.

Blocking: Using the body, arm or leg to stop or divert an attack.

Bo: A wooden staff of approximately 6 feet in length. Japanese term.

Bogu: Japanese "armor."

Bogu Kumite: "Sparring in armor." Used when practicing full contact.

Bojutsu: A Japanese martial art that emphasizes the use of the Bo(staff).

Bokken: A wooden sword used in Kenjutsu for training. It is shaped like the curved Samurai sword.

Boktu: A straight wooden sword used in some styles of Kenjutsu.

For example this is the type used in the Kashima-Shinden Jikishin-

Kage Ryu Kenjutsu style.

Breakfall:(Ukemi) Method of landing safely when thrown to the ground.

Breaking: (Tameshiwari) The method used to test striking power in karate by breaking a variety of material using various parts of the body.

Brave: A warror. The term the American Indians used for their warriors.

Budo: Japanese term for Martial Way. Designed to develop character by the practice of the martial arts.

Budoka: Martial way person. Someone who practices the martial ways.

Bujutsu: Japanese term applied to all the martial arts used to defeat a foe in battle. Designed primarily to win on the battle field.

Bushi: Japanese term for warrior up to the 15TH century, when the term Samurai became in use to honor Japan's warrrior class.

Bushido: Way of the warrior. A code of conduct Japan's Samurai were required to follow.

Bushi-FIST-Jujitsu: A jujitsu style founded by Joseph J. Truncale in 1985.

Chinna: Chinese art of seizing, which is a method of grappling thought to be the forerunner Jujitsu.

Choke: (Shime-waza) The grappling method used to stop an opponent's breathing or blood flow to the brain. Chudan: Japanese term for middle level of the body. Used in many martial art systems.

Chudan no-Kamae: Japanese term for middle level guard position used in Kendo and Kenjutsu.

Chudan Tsuki: Middle level strike to the stomach using a punch.

Chudan Uke: Middle level block.

Chui: A Warning given during competition.

Combination Techniques: Linking two or more techniques together into a sequence.

Dachi: "Position." The posture used during martial arts practice.

Daisho: "Big and small." Refers to the pair of swords carried by the Japanese Samurai.

Daito: The long samurai sword. It is also called the Katana.

Dan: Rank or grade in the martial arts. For example, a Shodan rank in a Japanese martial art means the person has attained a first Dan (degree).

De Ashi Bari: Advanced foot sweep throw used in Judo and Jujitsu.

Do: Japanese term for way or path.

Dogi: Martial way uniform; a tunic worn for practice.

Dojo: A term used for a Japanese training place to learn a martial art.

Empi: "Flying Swallow." A karate kata using large sweeping movements.

Empi uchi: "Elbow strike."

Escrima: Another name for Arnis de Mano.

Focus: A term used in the martial arts to explain a concentration of energy and force on impact.

Form: A term used to stress body position and a sequence of movements learning a martial art, as in kata.

Freestyle Sparring: The most advanced level, where students exchange techniques unrehearsed. Control is emphasized in this practice.

Front Kick: (Mae geri) The front kick is done by raising the knee and either snapping the front foot forward(Mae-geri-keagi) and back quickly, and by thrusting the foot forward(Mae-geri-kekomi).

Fuji, Mount: The most famous mountain in Japan, and climbed by thousands of people every year.

Full Contact: A method of fighting in which blows are delivered with full power against an opponent.

Fumikomi: "Step in." This is a stamping kick to the opponent's knee, shin, or instep.

Funakoshi, Gichin Considered by many to be the father of modern karate be-cause he was the first to bring the art to Japan from Okinawa in 1922. Though he did not give his style a name, preferring to just call it karate. His students began using his Pen name, "Shoto" to define the style and now it is known as Shotokan.

Garami: "Entanglement."

Gari: Reaping action to an opponent's leg used in throwing a subject in Judo and Jujitsu.

Gatame: Locking or holding a subject in Judo and Jujitsu practice.

Gedan barai: "Downward block."

Gedan tsuki: "Downward strike." A punch aimed at the lower stomach and groin area of an opponent's body.

Geri: "Kicking techniques."

Gi: The unform worn by martial arts students.

Goju ryu: "Hard/soft tradition." A karate style based on Shorei ryu and founded by Kannryo Higaonna.

Goshi: "Hip."

Goshinjutsu: Self defense techniques, and a style of jujitsu.

This is the style of the Judo self defense Kata.

Grappling Techniques: Martial arts that employ throws, locks and holds.

Ground work: Wrestling, judo and ju-

jitsu techniques applied on the ground.

Guard Position: Technique used in many grappling and self defense arts that makes use of the maximum amount of personal weapons, while giving the opponent little opportunity to use his weapons.

Gyaku mawshigeri: "Reverse roundhouse kick used in karate.

Gyaku tsuki: "Reverse punch."

Hachimaki: "Head wrapping." Cotton towel used around the forehead to keep sweat from the eyes.

Haiku: A Japanese form of poetry that employes just three lines, using a five-seven-five syllables. First created by Matsuo Basho(1644-1694), who was a teacher and master of the poetic form known as Renga.

Haito: "Ridge hand."

Hajime: Term used by Japanese meaning to "begin" sparring.

Hakama: "Split skirt." Loose flowing trousers used in many traditional martial arts as a uniform.

Hammer fist: A blow used with the little finger side of the closed fist.

Hanare: Point in Japanese archery at which the arrow is released.

Hanbo: A short wooden staff.

Hane goshi: "Spring hip throw."

Hane makikomi: "Outer winding spring hip throw." Used in Judo/Jujitsu.

Hangetsu: "Half moon.' A shorei ryu karate kata.

Hansoku: "Foul." as in a match.

Hanshi: Master; a very high rank of at least 8th dan.

Hantei: "Decision." A judging panel in a match.

Hapkido: A Korean martial art that is similar to Aikido and Jujitsu in that circular movements are emphasized.

Hara: "Abdomen." The area emphasized emphasized in many martial arts as the source of power.

Harai goshi: "Sweeping hip throw." Used in Judo and jujitsu.

Hari Kiri: An informal term for the Japanese ritual for committing suicide by slitting the belly.

Heel kick: A kick which uses the heel to strike an opponent.

Heian: "Peace." A series of five karate katas originated by Yasutsune Itosu. Usually the first katas a karate student learns in class.

Hidari: "Left." Term used in Kendo and Kenjutsu.

Hiza: "Knee."

Hiza guruma: "Knee Wheel," throw.

Hojo: The main Kenjutsu kata practiced by students of the Kashima-Shinden Jikishin-Kage Ryu.

Hojo Breathing: Special breathing exercises used in the Kashima-Shinden Jikishin-Kage Ryu Kenjutsu.

Hojo jutsu: The art of tying up an opponent using rope.

Hojutsu: The art of using firearms.

Hojo Walking: A special method of walking taught in the Kashima-Shinden Jikishin-Kage Ryu Kenjutsu.

Hold down: techniques used to secure your opponent to the ground.

Honbu: "Headquarters." A traditional schools main dojo.

Hung gar: A Kung Fu style.

Hwarang do: "Way of the flowering youth." A Korean warrior code of ethics and martial art.

Iaijutsu: The sword art of drawing the sword out quickly and cutting, and than placing the sword back in the sheath. Ibuki: Breath control method taught in some martial art systems.

Ippon: One point score in martial art competition.

Ippon seoi nage: "One arm shoulder throw." Used in judo and jujitsu.

Ippon shobu: "One point throw." Competition decided on a single full point. Used in karate and other arts.

Jigo hontai: Judo defensive position with both knees bents and the hips are lowered, making it difficult to throw an opponent.

Jikan: "Time." As in a expired match.

Jion: A karate kata named after the famous Buddhist temple at Jion-ji.

Jitte: "Ten hands." A karate kata.

Jiujitsu(also written Jujitsu and Jiujutsu): Compliant or gentle art. The original combat system from which most modern martial arts were born. This art included numerous unarmed and armed methods of combat. It is considered thc parent martial art of Judo, Karate, Aikido, and other combat systems.

Jiu Kumite: "Free sparring."

Jo: A staff usually measuring 4 to 5 feet in length. Used for practicing stick fighting in various self defense systems, including Jujitsu and Aikido.

Jodan: Upward: Shoulder, head and neck areas.

Jodan uke: "Upward block."

Jogai: "Out of bounds" as in a match.

Jojitsu: The art of using the staff.

Jonin: "an experienced ninja."

Judo: Gentle way: Developed by Jigoro Kano into a sport.

Throwing, ground grappling and chokes are emphasized in this art. It is also an Olympic sport.

Judogi: Judo uniform. Worn by those who practice judo.

Judoka: a person who practices judo.

Juji gatame: "Cross armlock."

Juji jime: "Cross choke lock." A choke hold in which a cross grip is employed on the opponent's collar.

Juji uke: "Cross block or X block."

Jutsu: A term that means "art" and refers to the tradition based upon true military practice.

Jutte: A forked iron trunheon.

Kakato: "the heel."

Kage: "Shadow."

Kama: "Sickle." One of the karate weapons of self defense. It has a handle and a hook like blade. It is used in pairs, in most cases.

Kamae: "Stance." It is a posture used during martial arts practice.

Kami basani: "Crab scissors." This is a sacrifice throw using the legs.

Kancho: "Grand master." Chief instructor of a karate school of style.

Kanku: "Looking to the sky." A karate black belt kata.

Kano, Jigoro: The founder of Judo. The person responsible for bringing judo to the world and creating the sport.

Kansetsu waza: "Locking techniques."

Karate: "Empty hand" or China hand. An Okinawan fighting system brought to Japan from Okinawa, where the meaning of the name changed at tht time. Gichin Funakoshi changed the name of the art from Karate jutsu to Karate do to reflect the spiritual and philoso-phical aspects of the art.

Karate Do: "Way of karate."

Karate Jutsu: "Art of Karate." Refers to the study of karate for practical combat purposes rather than sport.

Karate Ka: A person who practices, or is a student of karate.

Kashima: A shrine in Japan honoring ancient relatives of the past, and where a formal Kenjutsu(sword art) school was created.

Kata: "Formal Exercise." Pre-arranged exercises done to practice the techniques of a martial art. Can be done alone or with another student.

Kata gatame: "Shoulder hold." Properly applied this hold can also become a strangle technique.

Kata guruma: "Shoulder wheel throw." This throw is used in many jujitsu styles and is performed by placing the opponent on the shoulders to throw him/her.

Katana: "Sword." Refers to the long Samurai sword, also called Daito.

Keibo: "Wooden truncheon."

Keikogu: Half-point penalty in a karate match.

Kekomi: "Thrust." As in kicking.

Kempo: A karate style that began in China, where it is called Ch'uan Fa.

Kendo: "Way of the sword." A sport where a bamboo sword called a Shinai.

Kendoka: A person who practices the sport of kendo.

Kenjutsu: "Sword art." Techniques of practical swordsmanship and not a sport. The art the Samurai learned.

Kenshi: "Fencer."

Keri waza: "Kicking techniques."

Kesa gatame: "Scarf hold." Judo and jujitsu ground technique.

Kevlar: The material bullet resistant vests are made of that police wear.

Ki: "Spirit." Energy of the body, mind and spirit working together as one.

Kiai: "Spirit harmony." Joining the determination and will with physical action, usually expressed with a loud shout.

Kibadachi: "Straddle stance." This is also called the horse stance, as it appears the student is riding a horse when this stance is employed.

Kickboxing: A full contact sport utilizing the hands and feet.

Kihon: The fundamental or basic techniques of a martial art.

Kime: "Focus." Concentration of power in one specific area.

Kiritsu: "Stand." To return to your feet after a kneeling(Seiza) position. Knight: European warrior class.

Kobudo: The practice of martial arts, specifically weapons.

Kobojutsu: "Old martial art." Refers to the classical practice of the martial arts, specifically weapons.

Kodachi: "Small sword." Refers to the smaller of the two swords worn by the Samurai.

Kodokan: "Hall for teaching the way." Established by Jigoro Kano, the founder of Judo in 1882.

Kogusoku: One predecessor of jujitsu.

Kote: "Wrist." Used in kendo.

Kote waza: "Wrist locking technique."

Kung Fu: "Well done." Refers to many Chinese martial art systems today.

Kusarigama: "Chain and sickle." A Japanese martial art employing a multi-purpose weapon. One of the main weapons used by warrior monks.

Kwoon: Chinese and Korean term for training hall.

Kyokushinkai: "Way of ultimate truth." A karate style founded by Masutatu Oyama. A full contact hard karate style.

Kyoshi: "Teacher grade." Someone who has achieved at least 6th dan in a martial art.

Kyu: "Grade." Referred to as levels below black belt.

Kyudo: "Way of the bow." A Japanese art of using the bow.

Kyujutsu: "Art of the bow." Orginal art of using the bow in actual combat situations. The parent art of Kyudo.

Lee, Bruce: The founder of Jeet Kune do. Famous for his innovative ideas and approaches to practical combat.

Maai: "Distancing." Refers to the distance between two opponents.

Maigeri: "Front kick" in karate.

Maki komi: "Winding throw" used in judo and jujitsu where you wrap your body into the arm and body of your opponent, taking subject down.

Makiwara: "Straw padded post." Used for developing the hand and strikes.

Manriki Gusari: "Ten thousand power chain." A weighted chain at both ends that was used in combat.

Martial art: "Military techniques." Refers to techniques and methods used by the classical warrior, but now the term is used to describe any type of self defense art.

Mawashi geri: "Round house kick."

Mawashi tsuki: "Round house punch."

Meijin: "Expert." Refers to someone who has transcended techniques alone and has developed skill to an art form.

Men: Refers to the head protector used in Kendo. Used when the kendo player strikes the head area.

Migi: "Right" side technique.

Mizu no kokoro: "Mind like water." A zen term to indicate a calm and clear mind.

Mokuso: "Quiet thought." The beginning and ending meditation time used in many martial arts.

Monkey: One of the five animals on which a system of kung fu is based.

Morote tsuki: "Double punch."

Morote uke: "Double block."

Muay Thai: A full contact sport developed in Thailand and practiced around the world.

Nage waza: The throwing techniques of judo and jujitsu.

Naginata: "Reaping sword." It has a halberd with a sword blade attached to a long handle.

Naginata do: "Way of using the reaping sword." The practice of using the reaping sword. A popular martial art practiced by mostly Japanese women today.

Naginata jutsu: "Art of using the reaping sword." The orginal military use of this weapon.

Naha te: "Hand of Naha." The orginal name used in Okinawa for karate.

Ne waza: Ground techniques of judo and jujitsu.

Ninja: Hired spy or assassin.

Nippon kempo: "Japanese boxing." A martial art that used kendo type of equipment to spar full contact.

Nukite: "Spear hand" strike.

Nunchaku: "Wooden flair." A weapon made of two wooden sections with a cord or chain attaching them.

Odachi: "Great sword." A weapon worn together with the kodachi by Japanese samurai.

Oden: The Viking God of war.

Ogoshi: "Major hip throw."

Oguruma: "Major wheel" judo throw.

Oi tsuki: "Lunge punch."

Okinawa te: "Hand of Okinawa." Refers to all Okinawa karate. One step sparring: A karate method of training where an attacker throws one technique and the defender blocks and counters with another technique.

Osae Waza: "Holding techniques." Judo and jujitsu immobilizing methods.

O-Sensei: "Great teacher." In most cases the founder of a style of its chief instructor.

Osotogari: "Major outer reaping" judo and jujitsu throw.

Otoshi: "Drop" throw.

Pa kua: "Eight trigrams." One of the three internal schools of kung fu.

Palm heel: A thrusting strike using the palm of the hand.

Parry: "Deflecting a blow or kick."

Pattern: Another name for kata/form.

Penjak silat: The national martial art of Indonesia, which uses both unarmed and armed methods of combat.

Pinan: "Peaceful mind." This was the orginal name of the katas now known as the Heian katas and devised in 1903 by Yasutsune Itosu.

Randori: Judo free style practice.

Rank: refers to the level of proficiency gained in a system.

Reap: Wrapping your leg around your opponent's to throw the subject.

Rei: "Bow."

Renshi: "Accomplished person." Usually a 5th dan or higher.

Renshu: "Practice."

Rotashi, Sogen Oyori: Present leader of the Kashima-Shinden Jikishin-Kage Ryu Kenjutsu school.

Ryu: Traditional school or style.

Sai: A short handled trident which can also be used as a truncheon.

Samurai: "One who serves." The title of the Japanese warrior class.

Sanbon kumite: "Three step sparring."

Sanchin: Karate kata devised by Chojun Miyagi of the Goju ryu.

Sanchin dachi: "Hourglass stance."

Sankaku-jime: "Triangular necklock." A strangulation judo/jujitsu techni-que in which one of the opponent's arms is locked up with his/her neck.

Seiken: "Fore-fist."

Seisan: A Japanese kata named after the person who devised this form.

Seiza: "correct sitting." The formal kneeling position in the martial arts.

Sempai: "Senior." Refers to senior person in relationships.

Sensei: "Teacher."

Seoi nage: "Shoulder throw" used in judo and jujitsu.

Seppuku: Formal name for Harigari, or ritual suicide.

Shaolin: Famous Buddhist monastery associated with martial art practice. It is still in existence in a rebuilt form.

Shiai jo: "Contest place." Used to mean where a contest is taking place.

Shihan: "Supreme teacher." The head of a school, style or tradition.

Shimewaza:"Strangulation techniques." Judo and jujitsu chokes and strangles. Shimpan: "Referee."

Shin: Leader in Hojo kata.

Shito ryu: Japanese style of karate founded by Kenwa Mabuni.

Shizentai: "Natural position." A relaxed yet ready stance in which one foot slightly leads the other.

Shorei ryu: Okinawan style of karate developed orginally from Naha-te.

Shorinji kempo: "Shaolin Temple boxing."

Shorin ryu: One of the styles of Okinawan karate.

Shotokan: Gichin Funakoshi's pen name and the name of his karate club. First to be invited and bring the art of karate to Japan.

Shuai chiao: A style of Chinese wrestling.

Shugyo: "Intense training." This type of training is done once or twice a year by many martial arts. It can last from a few days to a week.

Shukokai: A style of karate developed by a student of Mubuni(founder of Shito-ryu) named Chojiro Tani.

Shurikan: A sharp edged throwing star used mostly by the ninjas.

Shuri te: One of the orginal Okinawan karate styles.

Shute: "Knife hand." Edge of hand.

Side kick: Using the side and heel of the foot to kick.

Sifu: "Teacher." Chinese name.

Silat: "Fast action." An Indonesian martial art in which unarmed and armed techniques are employed.

Snap kick: A technique in which to kick is thrown and retrieved in a quick snapping action.

Sojutsu: "Japanese spear art."

Sokaku, Takeda: Master swordsman and master of the famous traditional Daito ryu aikijujutsu, which is the fore-runner of Aikido.

Sokuto: "Knife foot." Little toe edge of the foot.

Soto uke: "Outside block."

Sparring: An exchange of techniques with students.

Spartans: Greek warriors from Sparta who were trained from birth in the warrior arts. They were known for their intense training and spirit.

Spear hand: Hand weapon which thrusts the extended fingers into the target.

Special forces: Specialized group within an armed service that receive intense training in combat methods. Every armed service has these unique fighting people in their branches.

Staff: Wooden pole about 6 feet long.

Stamping kick: A technique in which the heel is driven downward into a target.

Stance: A posture or position used in all martial arts.

Sticking hands: A method of sparring used in Wing Chun Kung Fu.

Straddle stance: Another name for horse stance. (Kiba dachi)

Style: Refers to the school or martial art method being practiced.

Suiei jutsu: "Swimming art." The art of swimming used by warriors.

Sumo: An ancient and still popular form of Japanese wrestling.

Sutemi waza: "Sacrifice technique" throw used in judo and jujitsu.

Sweep: Displacing the opponent's supporting foot to cause a loss of balance.

Sweet Science: American term for the art of boxing.

Tachi: An ancient Japanese long sword that was replaced by the Katana sword.

Taekwondo: "Kick/punch way." The Korean art of using the hands and feet for self defense and sport.

Tai Chi Chuan: "Great ultimate fist." One of the Chinese martial arts.

Taiho jutsu: "Arrest techniques." Police techniques of arrest and control taught in Japan.

Tai jutsu: "Body art." The prede-
cessor of jujitsu.

Tai otoshi: "Body drop." A judo throw in which an opponent is thrown over an extended leg.

Tai sabaki: "Body movement." Used to refer to methods to evade an attack.

Tameshiwari: "To test by breaking." The method of breaking wood, tiles and bricks to test power.

Tanden: "Abdomen." The center of gravity and power that all martial arts emphasize.

Tang soo do: "Way of the tang hand." A Korean martial art that teaches how to use the hand and foot for combat.

Tanto: Single edged Japanese knife.

Tatami: "Mat." Used in judo, jujitsu and other martial arts.

Te: "Hand."

Teisoku: "Sole of foot."

Tekki: "Horse riding." A set of three katas derived from Naihanchi.

Tensyo: A training kata devised by Gojo ryu karate fonder Chojun Miyagi.

Thai boxing: "Muay Thai." A full contact sport and art developed and practiced in Thailand.

Tomari te: One of the older Okinawan karate schools. Now called Shuri te.

Tomoe nage: "Circle throw." One of the sacrifice throws of judo and jujitsu, in which the foot is planted on the uke's stomach and wheels him/her over the body.

Tonfa: "Handle." An Okinawan karate weapon of self defense.

Tori: "Taker." The person who performs the technique on his partner. The one who defends and counters an attack in most cases.

Tsuki: "Thrust" type of technique.

Tsuke waza: "Punching techniques."

Uchi: A "Strike" in which the hand is partially or fully open.

Uchimata: "Inner thigh throw."

Ude: "Forearm."

Ude garami: "Entangled armlock." A judo lock that works against the elbow joint.

Ude uke: "Forearm block."

Uechi ryu: An Okinawan style of karate founded by Kanbun Uechi.

Uke: 1. Block. 2. Person who receives Tori's technique. Usually the person who initiates the attack in judo or jujitsu. The Tori counters the attack.

Ukemi: "Art of falling." Judo and Jujitsu techniques of falling.

Uraken: "Reverse fist." (Back fist)

Ushiro geri: "Back kick."

Uyeshiba, Morihei: The honorable founder of Aikido. Referred to by students as O'Sensei.

Vajramushti: An early Indian martial art of which no trace can now be found.

Wado ryu: "Way of harmony tradition." A karate style founded by Hironori Ohtsuka.

Wakizashi: "Short sword." The shorter sword worn with the Katana.

Waza: "Technique."

Wing Chun: A Chinese style of kung fu developed by the Buddhist monk Nun Ng Mui. This was the art Bruce Lee first learned from Yip Man.

Wu shu: "Martial art." The martial arts of the Chinese mainland.

X-block: Blocking an attack with crossed forearms.

Yama zuki: "Combined punch" in which a double thrust or strike is made with both of the hands.

Yamei: "Halt." Command to stop training.

Yari: "Spear."

Yoko geri: "Side kick."

Yudansha: "Black belt holder."

Zanshin: "Alert posture." Maintaining alertness during practice.

Zen: A Buddhist system often related to the practice of the martial arts. It is not a religion per se, but a method to achieve a calm mind. It is often related to the practice of martial arts in many countries.

Zenkutsudachi: "Forward stance" used in karate.

ABOUT THE AUTHOR

Joseph J. Truncale has been a lifetime student of the martial arts. He first took up wrestling and boxing in 1956 and joined the U.S. Navy in 1959. In 1961 he began his training in Judo and Karate while stationed in Japan aboard the USS Oklahoma City, a guided missle cruiser. He continued his training in Judo and Karate while in the Navy until his honorable discharge in 1963. He kept seeking out more martial arts knowledge, joining a Shotokan Karate club under Mr. Sugiyama, Sensei, who was the chief instructor of all Midwest Shotokan Karate.

In 1965 he joined the Glenview, Ill Police Department, and also studied Judo at the Glenview Judo club at that time. He also continued his Shotokan Karate training under Mr. Copeland, Sensei, who was also a student of Mr. Sugiyama. When Mr. Copeland moved from the area, Mr. Truncale continued his training under Mr. Rogers, Sensei, who also had been a student of Mr. Sugiyama. At that time, Mr. Truncale also attended numerous police arrest and control seminars, becoming a certified instructor in many systems. He has been involved in the martial arts for more than 40 years, studying many combat and weapon systems under numerous excellent instructors. He has earned Black Belts in Karate(5th Dan-USMA), Judo (5th Dan-USMA), Jujitsu (9th Dan-USMA) and Kobudo (3rd Dan).

In 1973 Mr. Truncale, Sensei, founded the first Karate club in Glenview at the Glenview Playdium and the Glenview Park Dist., which was also one of the first Karate clubs on the entire northshore of Chicago at that time. He also founded the first Jujitsu club in Glenview on the Glenview Naval Air Station around 1980, as well as the first Jujitsu club at the Glencoe Park District around that same time period.

Though Mr. Truncale has worked in many areas of law enforcement, his special expertise is in the police defensive tactics and police weapon fields. He has designed numerous police survival courses and has taught police and security officers from all over the world at international seminars. He is a certified International Instructor in the PR-24 Police Baton, the MEB (Monadnock Exp. Straight Baton) program, the Monadnock Defensive Tactics System (MDTS), and the Persuader (small stick) Baton. He is also certified as a Master Instructor in the CLAMP, the GRASP, and OC Spray. He has had the honor to have studied from some of the best minds and most talented martial art and police instructors in the world. (SEE SPECIAL THANKS AND ACKNOWLEDGMENTS FOR LIST)

He is the founder (Soke) of BUSHI SATORI RYU, a jujitsu style which blends the traditional Samurai arts with modern combat methods. The learning of 16 martial art weapons and 12 police weapons are part of his system. He has also created SAMURAI AEROBICS and PERSUADER DEFENSE SYSTEMS. He has had more than 400 papers (articles, essays, poems and reviews) and 35 books/manuals published. He also writes several columns and has his own newsletter, The Samurai Heart. He is one of the founding directors of The American Society for Law Enforcement Training (ASLET), and is on the advisory board of the International Law Enforcement Educators and Trainers Association, The Illinois Police Instructor's Association, and the Monadnock Police Training Council.

He is a member of numerous professional associations (ILEETA, ASLET, IPITA, USJA, USMAA, IAPJ). He offers more than 40 police and civilian self defense courses. He teaches a college credit course in Police Tactics at Oakton Com. College, and also teaches Jujitsu at the Lattorf YMCA in DesPlaines, Ill with other high ranking black belts. He is available on a select basis, for seminars and private lessons. Contact: Pro-Systems & Bushi Satori Ryu: P.O. Box 261, Glenview, Ill 60025-0261.

Phone/Fax: 847/729-7681.
WEB SITE: www.samuraiway.com
E-Mail: pro-bushi@webtv.net

www.ingramcontent.com/pod-product-compliance
Ingram Content Group UK Ltd.
Pitfield, Milton Keynes, MK11 3LW, UK
UKHW041942190726
13854UKWH00004B/1740